D1523330

OSSIE:
The
Autobiography
of a
Black Woman

OSSIE:
The
Autobiography
of a
Black Woman

by Ossie Guffy

as told to Caryl Ledner

W · W · NORTON & COMPANY · INC ·

NEW YORK

Copyright © 1971 by Bantam Books, Inc.

First Edition

SBN 393 07458 7

Library of Congress Catalog Card No. 74-141940

All Rights Reserved
Published simultaneously in Canada
by George J. McLeod Limited, Toronto

Designed by Ruth Smerechniak

PRINTED IN THE UNITED STATES OF AMERICA

1 2 3 4 5 6 7 8 9 0

TO

Susan Evanns,

who brought us together.

A social worker with soul.

PREFACE

This may seem like a strange book, like a voice out of the past. During this turbulent time of the emergence of the black American from the shadow world into which he has been pushed by white society, it isn't stylish to talk about black life as it has been lived by the majority of black people. Books are being written by the dozen on the sociological, psychological, and economic plight of blacks en masse, and more books are being written by black men, writing subjectively about the hell of the ghetto, drug addiction, crime, and degradation. This is a book unlike any of these. It is subjective, but its protagonist is neither male nor degraded. Rather, it is the personal history of one black woman, growing up in the less dramatic but more usual world of lower-middle-class America, in the period from 1931 to the present.

I was introduced to Ossie Guffy in the fall of 1967 by a social worker who recognized in Ossie the real spirit of the black woman in America. Ossie was, and still is, what the welfare people euphemistically refer to as a "client." She herself was not receiving aid, but of her nine children, the five who were born to her before she married Clarence Guffy were, and are, on Aid to Dependent Children.

When we met, we liked each other immediately, and we both felt that we would like to spend a little time together getting to know each other and that, if at the end of that time we both wanted it, I would try to get Ossie's story down on paper. We both wanted it, and this is the result.

Ossie talked, and I wrote, and I've tried to keep to her words and her thoughts. I've added continuity and some organization; but the thoughts and the feelings and the reactions are Ossie— a woman who is black.

INTRODUCTION

I'M A WOMAN, I'M BLACK, I'M A LITTLE UNDER FORTY, AND I'M
more of black America than Ralph Bunche or Rap Brown or
Harry Belafonte, because I'm one of the millions who ain't
bright, militant, or talented. The poor sections of every city
and town are filled with people like me, black and white, who
start every day wondering if the money'll make it through
the week and if they'll have the strength to keep on trudging
up a hill that ain't got no top and knowing, while they're
wondering, that they've had the strength up to now and they'll
probably keep right on having it.

I've been on welfare, but I ain't never been on dope; I got
more children than I can rightly take care of, but I ain't got
more than I can love; I've worked until I fell over and then
got up and worked again—and I ain't one whit different than
most of my neighbors. We're the women you got used to seeing in your kitchens and the men you got used to seeing as
Red Caps, dining-car waiters, day laborers—the people who
lived over on the other side of town. We lived there and we
suffered there and we died there, and we did all three quietly.
But now that time is past, and it ain't never going to come

9

back. It may be better than it was, it may be worse than it was, but one thing's for sure—it ain't going to be the same as it was.

Your TV screens are showing more black faces, and you're reading about us in your papers, but you ain't getting any picture of what we're really like, 'cause most of us ain't got any voices speaking for us. I don't think most whites are like Richard Nixon or Lucy or George Wallace, and most blacks ain't like Dick Gregory or Julia or Muhammad Ali. Most whites are like you, and most blacks are like me.

The educated ones all say we're at a crossroads, and where we're going is anybody's guess. I sure don't know the answer to that one, but I *do* know one thing—to get any place at all, we're all going to have to get to know each other a little better than we do. I got a lot of kids growing up, and I guess you do, too, and I sure hope they have a chance to be the best they can be. So I'm going to try to tell it like it was, hoping it will throw a little light on the millions of us that ain't been rightly seen before. I sure wish some of you'd do the same for us.

OSSIE:
The
Autobiography
of a
Black Woman

· 1 ·

A WHITE LADY WHO REALLY WANTED TO KNOW ONCE ASKED ME, "How does it feel to be born black?" I didn't answer her question because I didn't know how, but I never forgot it, and now that I want so much to tell what it's like to *be* black it's come back to my mind.

I guess you can't say what it's like to be *born* black, because when you're born—and for a long time after—you don't know you *are* black. When you look in a mirror, you see a little girl with dark skin, but it doesn't mean anything special to you, because when you're little you haven't learned yet that the color of your skin is going to be the most important fact of your life, the prison that locks you out instead of in, the package around your soul that sets up an immediate reaction in the white world and makes you forever an inferior, unless proven otherwise. No, when you're very young, you're just Ossie, a little girl with one brother and three sisters, a mother who doesn't live with you but visits every Thursday and every other Sunday, and no father.

I was born on March 10, 1931, in Walnut Hills, a Negro suburb of Cincinnati, Ohio. At the time of my birth, my mother, then twenty-two, had already had a boy and two girls, all a year apart. My father, Gray, was twenty-seven. He was a candy maker and he brought home a pay check large enough for us all to live on comfortably. We had our own house, which we rented, plenty to eat, lots of warmth when it was cold outside, and a big back yard to play in when the weather was fine. It was a real middle-class house with inside plumbing, doors that hung straight, windows that weren't broken, and a roof that never leaked. My mother didn't have to go out to work then, and she stayed home and took care of all of us, and though I was too little to remember it, my brother told me later it was like heaven because my mother was so young and so pretty and the house was so nice.

I never got to know it like that, because when I was thirteen months old my father died of an asthma attack. I have a picture of him, taken just before his death, and sometimes, when I look at it, I'm glad he died when he did. He looks so young and innocent and kind of guileless . . . I don't think he could have stood what happened later.

At the time of my father's death, my mother was pregnant again. There she was, young, scared, with four children and another on the way, and no money. Like all of us, she did what she had to do. Although she had never gotten along with her father, she got him and her mother to come live with us and she hired out as a maid. At first she refused to take a job if she had to live in, because that meant being away from us children most of the time, but pretty soon she could see that she couldn't make ends meet doing day work. Besides, if she lived in, she got her room and board for nothing, and that helped, too.

She did day work until my baby sister was born, and then, when the baby was two weeks old, she got a good job with a nice family and moved out. She used to come to see us on her days off, every Thursday and every other Sunday, and these days were like holidays to us. When she came she would bring us candy, do our hair, clean us up, and sometimes even take us to the park or for a ride on the bus.

Not that my grandma didn't keep us clean and all. She did,

but somehow when my mother did my hair or washed my face it was like I was a princess, because she made it so plain that I was important and how I looked was important too. My grandma said it was wrong to be dirty, but my mama said it was beautiful to be clean. Looking back, I guess Mama treated all us kids the same, but somehow she made each one feel the most important.

Grandma really had her hands full. She went out to work early every morning and didn't get home until dark. Then she cooked dinner for us all, washed up, and did the housework she hadn't had time for in the morning. It's shocking to realize that my grandma at that time was only about four years older than I am now. How come I'm a young woman and Grandma was an old lady?

Grandpa was left in charge of us all. In those days he called himself a victim of the Depression, which no doubt he was, but the Depression wasn't the only force that had laid him low. He was a good man, an honest man, but, unfortunately, like many black men he was weak. He had no education, but he had learned a trade at an early age and when he worked, he worked in construction as a cement spreader. Before the Depression, from what I've heard, he divided his time equally between working and drinking. When the really hard times hit, he worked on the WPA fitfully and spent the rest of the time taking care of us and sneaking off around the corner to the saloon whenever he could escape Grandma.

Grandma didn't know she was strong. She just knew she had to do what she had to do, so she did it and found out it could be done. Grandpa didn't know he was weak. He just thought he couldn't do what he had to do, so what was the use in trying? Besides, Grandma always saw to it that, somehow, the family survived. Lots of black people fall back on the comforting thought that the Lord will provide. To a black man, I suspect that the Lord is a black woman.

Anyway, there we were, Mama living out, Grandma working, and Grandpa taking care of us. I guess it might have gone on that way a lot longer, except for what happened to Delia. Alice, my oldest sister, was seven, and Verne, my brother, was eight, and they were in school. The rest of us were too young, and we stayed home with Grandpa, doing the little chores that Grandma gave us, but mostly playing. We were all pretty good kids, but we were very young, and Grandpa slept a lot, so we got into mischief, but it was mostly harmless. Delia, who was six, was usually the one who made up the games we played. She was very good at imagining things and she remembered every line out of every book that Mama ever read to us, so we let her lead.

This one day, everything seemed to go wrong from the beginning. It was a Thursday in February and it was cold, and I mean cold. We had a big pot-bellied stove in the middle of the kitchen, and it was Grandpa's job to keep enough wood cut and stacked so we could keep the fire blazing. When Grandma got up at six o'clock, she'd start the stove, and by the time we had had breakfast the kitchen was warm and cozy. Well, this particular day it seemed that no matter how much wood Grandma fed that big old stove, the kitchen just wouldn't warm up. By the time she was ready to leave for work the wood basket was nearly empty, and she told Delia to be sure and tell Grandpa, when he woke up, to get some wood right away. About an hour later, Grandpa came shuffling out of his room with his usual hangover. We knew from experience that when Grandpa first got up it was useless to talk to him, but it was getting colder and colder in the kitchen, and Delia was a determined little kid. She waited until he had his first sip of coffee and then she started.

"Grandma said you should get some more wood right away," she said firmly.

He didn't even turn his head. She decided to push on and repeated the sentence. He still didn't answer. Finally, she walked up to where he was standing and tugged on his pants-leg.

"Grandpa!" she practically yelled. "Grandma said you was to get some wood. It's cold in here!"

He still didn't answer, but I guess he must have heard, 'cause like he was sleepwalking, he went back in his room, put on his coat, and went out.

Time went by. It kept getting colder and colder, and still no sign of Grandpa with the wood. We all just kind of huddled around the stove. Finally Delia, the leader, announced that she knew a way we might keep warm. She told us how in a story Mama had read her, people made torches out of straw, and she figured if we each had our own torch we'd be warmer. We didn't have any straw, but Delia said we could try to make one torch out of the broom and if that worked, maybe we could figure out something else to burn.

With the rest of us as audience, Delia went and got the broom. Then she took the hot-pad to protect her hand and opened the heavy door on the big stove. Inside, the flames were crackling and sputtering, and the heat felt so good we all got as close as we could.

What happened after that happened so fast that even now it runs through my mind's eye like an old movie going double-quick. One minute Delia was holding the wooden handle of the broom and poking the straw end into the open door, the next a sheet of flame roared along the length of the broom and onto the sleeves of Delia's sweater, and from there she just seemed to go up in flames like the torch she was trying to make. I guess we all started to scream, and from somewhere Mama appeared and threw Delia down on the floor and rolled her over and over in the rug. Then she picked her up, rug and all, and ran out the front door. In a couple of minutes the lady from next door came over, and she stayed with us a while, but Mama and Delia didn't come back.

Late in the afternoon, Grandma came home, stayed a few minutes, and went out again. The lady from next door kept going back to her own house and then coming back to ours. Finally, she gave us our dinner and said we should go to bed. We were all frightened and cold, so the four of us got into bed together so that the warmth of our bodies heated each other up, and finally, we went to sleep.

Later, much later, when it seemed like the middle of the night to me, I woke up because I heard loud voices in the kitchen. At first I was too sleepy to really listen and I started to drift off again, but then my mother's steadily rising voice filled the room.

". . . one thing to be drunk all the time when it's just you, but Jesus! How could you do this to my kids? Babies, that's all they are, babies, and you went off to your lousy saloon and left them! You're a murderer, that's what you are, a murderer!"

"Betty Jo," pleaded my grandma, "honey, don't talk like that to your daddy. Delia's mighty bad, I know, but she ain't dead."

"She's going to be dead!" screamed my mother. "The doctor says she has terrible burns over most of her body and she's going to be dead, and he killed her!"

There was a short, sharp sound of flesh meeting flesh, and I heard my mother gasp.

"You don't talk about your daddy that way!" I heard my grandma's voice, deeper and more frightening than I ever remembered it. "You have some respect!"

My mother started to laugh, not a nice laugh like she used when she was happy, but a kind of sharp yelpy sound that was scary to listen to.

"Respect! Respect for what? Respect for who?" She kind of cried and laughed at the same time.

"Respect for my dear old daddy, who drank up the money you made by scrubbing other people's kitchens? Respect for my lovin' father who didn't care how hard you worked as long as he didn't? Respect for the granddaddy who let his granddaughter burn up while he was off drinking? You know where he'd be if it wasn't for you? Sleeping it off in some drunk tank downtown, that's where he'd be!"

Silence.

"If you feel that way about me," my grandpa said unsteadily, "how come you asked me to come help you out when Gray died?"

"You! Who wanted you? It was Mama I needed, it's always Mama I needed. You just came along for the ride. God help anybody who needs you!"

"That's enough!" said my grandma fiercely. "You just shut your mouth. I'm crying inside right along with you and your daddy 'bout Delia, but that ain't no reason to talk like you're talking. If you don't know by now that a black woman can get a job when a black man can't, you got a lot to learn. And natchully, he turns to the drink when he can't get nothing to bring home to his family. You ain't no man. You don't know how your daddy feels, so you just stop talking like that."

Then, like a dam had broken, the sound of my mother's sobs filled my ears.

"My baby . . . my little Delia . . . oh, Mama, my poor baby!"

"There, there," my grandma soothed. "You got to be strong. The Lord gives us the strength to face what we gotta face."

My mother stopped crying.

"If that's true, Mama," she said accusingly, "how come he only gives it to women?"

I became aware that I was cold and I was frightened, and I started to whimper, but nobody heard me. I didn't, I couldn't know it then, but I was starting my education as a black woman.

· 2 ·

DELIA DIDN'T DIE RIGHT AWAY. SHE LINGERED ON IN THE HOSPITAL, fighting for her life, but losing the battle day by day. After that awful night when I heard my mama and my grandpa fighting, they hardly spoke to each other at all, and Mama was so busy working and going to see Delia that we saw her even less. Life seemed to go on like before, except that Grandpa watched us better and Grandma didn't smile as much.

Then, one Sunday about five weeks after Delia's burning, Mama told us she had arranged for me and Janet, my baby sister, to go live with Aunt Mary. Alice was going to stay with Grandma 'cause she went to school and wasn't around the house all day, and Verne was going south to Georgia to live with my daddy's mama and papa. At first, when we heard what Mama said, it sounded exciting and different, but then we realized we were going to be separated, and that upset us. Mama didn't seem to pay any mind to how we felt about it, and we thought it was mean, but now I can see why she acted that way.

She knew it had to be done, and all our crying couldn't

change the necessity, so she stayed strong by pretending not to care how we felt.

Aunt Mary, who was Grandma's sister, lived about ten miles away from Walnut Hills in an area that was always referred to as "The Other Side of the Hill." If it had another name, I never heard it. It was right on the edge of Woptown, and there were some poor Italians living mixed in with the colored people. The whole place was owned by Italian businessmen, and they were our landlords.

Aunt Mary, who was a widow in her late thirties, considered herself much better off than her Italian neighbors, 'cause when Janet and I came to live with her, there were just the three of us in her two-room house, and that gave us plenty of room. All the houses were exactly alike, all clapboard, all old, all with only two rooms, and some of the poor Italian families had fourteen or fifteen kids, not to mention grandmas and grandpas and sometimes even great-grandparents. There was an outhouse behind every house and no fences, so it was pretty hard to grow anything or even keep grass, 'cause everybody walked on it.

Times were very hard then, and most of the people on The Other Side of the Hill kept alive just by refusing to die. A government truck came around once a month and gave each family a ration of staples—beans, flour, crackers, peanut butter, and the like. The people in the neighborhood called it the John Clark truck, and it wasn't until years later that I found out why. John Clark was the name of a trucking company that contracted with the federal government to make the food deliveries, but as far as I and, I think, most of the people in the neighborhood were concerned, John Clark was a kind man who wanted to help people in need. With what the truck brought as a base, everybody tried to earn a little money whatever way they could, and that wasn't easy or even always possible.

That same Sunday that Mama told us we were moving, she packed what few clothes we had, ignored our tears, and hustled us out and onto the bus. On the long ride to The Other Side of the Hill, she told us about Aunt Mary and her family, and it did help some, but we were still pretty upset. Looking back now, I realize how lucky we were that Aunt Mary existed.

She was probably the sweetest, kindest lady that ever lived, but Janet and I stayed kind of scared of her for a while, because she only had one leg. We couldn't figure out where she kept the other one, and we were always watching her to see if we could catch a glimpse of where she had it stashed. I guess at the beginning she was so busy trying to make us feel at home she didn't notice our curiosity, and after a little while we started accepting her the way she was.

She had three children of her own, but two were grown and lived away. The third, Cousin Robbie, worked as a sweep-up boy in a bar, even though he was only thirteen, and he lived in 'cause that way he got room and board, so Aunt Mary had been by herself for a while. She took in washing and ironing and managed to make about fifteen dollars a week from it, so when Mama asked her to look after us and said she'd help pay expenses, Aunt Mary agreed right away. The kind of woman she was, she would have taken us in and fed and loved us even if Mama couldn't pay.

It was a sight to see, the way she managed those crutches. She kept the house spotless and swung herself around like she didn't weigh anything at all. Most of the day she was washing and ironing, and she managed that by putting down one crutch and standing over the tub or the ironing board with the other one tucked under her arm. I'm sure there must have been times when she got discouraged and fed up, but she sure didn't show it. She had a smile and a word for everybody and, as far as I know, the only living thing in the whole world she couldn't abide was rabbits, 'cause her husband had been carried off in his twenties as the result of being bitten by a rabid rabbit while on a hunting trip.

That first Sunday she was waiting for us with a good dinner. First, she showed us the bedroom that Janet and I were to have for our very own, and that cheered us up some, 'cause we had never had anything of our very own before. Then she introduced us to Prunilla, a fat old hairy mutt that Aunt Mary loved like she was her own child. It was a funny thing with that dog; she was old and she was slow, and everybody could see it except Aunt Mary. As far as she was concerned, Prunilla was a frisky young thing and had to be babied. Sometimes I used to hear Mama teasing Aunt Mary about that dog, but she always had an answer.

"You are really something," Mama would say. "When you go about raising kids, you got a real good head on your shoulders, but when it comes to that dog you act like a fool. Taking on so with a dumb animal! It's downright silly."

Aunt Mary would shake her head at Mama. "You don't understand about dogs," she would say seriously. "When you're bringing up young ones you got to remember that being too soft ain't gonna help them to grow up and live in *this* world, but dogs are different. With a dog, you can be as silly as you want, 'cause all he ever has to be is a dog."

By the time we finished dinner on that first night, what with the excitement of moving and the amount of food we had tucked away, we were pretty sleepy. Mama washed us in the tin washtub that doubled as a wash basin, bathtub, and the place where Aunt Mary washed the clothes. There was no electricity in the house, and Aunt Mary used coal-oil lamps. They gave off a funny smell and a scary light, and it took me a while to get used to them. She led us into the bedroom, and when we were undressed she and Mama both tucked us in. We fell asleep right away, and everything would have been all right except that I woke up in the middle of the night because I had to go to the bathroom.

The house was pitch-black and ice-cold and deadly quiet. I wanted my mama and I knew she wasn't there and I was afraid to get out of bed and I didn't know what to do, so I tried to wake Janet. I never saw a little kid, then or now, who could sleep as deep as she did, and the more I poked her, the less result I got. She just rolled away from me and curled up in a little ball. I was getting panicky, between my need to go to the bathroom and my fear, and when she just wouldn't wake up I leaned over and bit her, hard, on the shoulder.

That did it, and she woke up screaming. When she realized she wasn't back home she screamed even louder. When I heard her yell, I guess it was too much for me, too, and I started sobbing like my heart would break. The noise reached Prunilla, who was in the front room, and she ran in and started barking, and it must have sounded like all hell broke loose. Into the middle of all this ruckus came the one thing sure to send Janet and me into hysterics. Delia used to tell us kids ghost stories, and she always described the ha'nts as kind of wavy white things that moved funny, and here, coming through the door, was a light that reflected on a wavy white thing, and it moved with thumps and groans. Janet got so scared she shut up, and I, of course, let loose and covered the bed with warm liquid, and generally it was a mess.

The white light approached the bed and attached to it was Aunt Mary's comforting brown face. She glared at Prunilla.

"You get on out of here!" she said sternly. "Ain't you ashamed, waking up my two little girls with your frisky ways? Making all that noise, it's enough to scare a body to death! Now git!"

Prunilla kind of scrunched down into herself and slunk out the door, and Aunt Mary turned her attention to us.

"Kind of scary, waking up in a strange place, ain't it? And then to have that animal howling in your ear! My, my, I guess I'd cry, too."

Janet pointed an accusing finger at me. "She bit me, and she peed in the bed. I'm all wet."

"Well, now," said Aunt Mary comfortably, "it's a good thing it's Monday, ain't it? We can throw them wet sheets right in with the other wash. C'mon now, you two. Get out of that bed. Monday's a mighty busy day around here."

I was about to say it was the middle of the night when I realized that while all the shouting had been going on the room had stopped being so black.

"You all know how to dress yourselves?" Aunt Mary wanted to know.

"I do, but Janet don't." Suddenly I felt important and grown up. "But I can dress her."

"That sure would be a help. I knew just looking at you that you was smart."

I guess maybe that was my first compliment, and it meant a lot to me. From then on I always tried as hard as I could not to let Aunt Mary change her mind about me, and I like to think she never did. The only place I didn't try as hard as I could was with the bed-wetting, 'cause getting out of a warm bed on a cold night and having to go freezing into the scary dark outside was worse than not being a good girl. I kind of think Aunt Mary understood, 'cause she didn't come down on me too hard about it, and Janet slept so deep she didn't hardly know the difference anyhow.

Those two years that we lived in that two-room shack passed pretty quick. Janet and I mostly played with each other, 'cause there weren't many kids our age around there, and we always had Thursdays and every other Sunday to look forward to, when Mama came to visit. Things were tough for everybody then, but in some ways we were lucky. Mama had a steady job, and what with the money she gave and the money Aunt Mary earned with the washing and ironing, we mostly had enough. Most months when the John Clark came around, Aunt Mary took her share and then divided it among the neighbors, black and white. That's one thing you gotta say for poor folks. They're hardly ever tight-fisted with each other.

At the beginning when Mama came and visited us she came alone, but after a little while John started coming with her. John was the other servant in the big house where she worked, and he and Mama were together a lot. He was about five years older than her and real nice-looking and very good to us. He brought presents and he played with us and he never tried to hustle Mama off, but just seemed happy to spend his time off lounging around Aunt Mary's house and having fun with us kids. I don't rightly know if *he* was having fun, but we sure were.

I guess it was a real good thing that John was around when Delia finally died. She'd been in the hospital about six months, sometimes more dead than alive, and just when the doctors thought she might make it, she developed pneumonia and died. I think Mama had expected her to die all along, and then things began to look better for Delia, and that was the cruelest part of all. Mama let herself hope, and then Delia died, and somehow she didn't have no way to defend herself from the sorrow. She just kind of wilted, and I think she would have given up, but John wouldn't let her. He gave her the support and the strength she needed, and as time went by she began to be her old self again.

After Mama and John had gone together about a year, they decided to get married and they came over one Sunday to tell us about it. I don't know if we would have been that excited, because as far as we were concerned they were as good as married anyhow, but the whole thing got better because John said that after he and Mama were married he would help Aunt Mary afford a better house with more rooms, where Mama and he could come and spend the night if they wanted to, and that's how come we left the two-room shack.

Our new house was still in the same general neighborhood, but it had three bedrooms and real electric lights and an inside bathroom. We moved in August, and in September Alice came to live with us, and she was real unhappy about it. She had always lived with Grandma, and that's where she wanted to stay, but that old bugaboo, necessity, had gotten mixed up in things again. I was old enough to start school that September, and school was pretty far away, and Mama and Aunt Mary didn't think I was big enough to go so far alone. Aunt Mary just couldn't navigate well enough to take me, so she and Mama decided that the only thing to do was to get Alice living with us, and then the two of us could go to school together. As I said, Alice liked it where she was and she didn't take kindly to the idea of being moved, and of course she blamed it all on me. Added to that, Janet and Alice and I shared a room and a big bed, and I had gotten so much in the habit of wetting the bed that I couldn't seem to stop even when the bathroom was indoors. Added together, I guess Alice felt she had a couple of pretty good reasons to hate me, and did she ever! She never missed a single chance to get me in trouble, she made my life at home as miserable as possible, and I don't know what I would have done if it hadn't been for the weekends. She was so lonely for Grandma and she carried on so about it that she conned John into taking her to Grandma's after school on Friday and bringing her back Sunday night, and that made three people very happy—Grandma and Alice and me. It's funny the way there are always some close people in your life that you live with like you're sisters, but inside the two of you are as strange to each other as if you'd never even met. That's the way it was with Alice and me then, and that's the way it's always stayed.

With Mama and John both giving money, and with times a little easier than they had been, life got better for all of us and particularly for Aunt Mary. Cousin Robbie got promoted to bartender, which he oughtn't to, 'cause he wasn't legally old enough, but he did, and he started giving Aunt Mary money. And with that and what she earned and what Mama and John gave, she was able to buy a washing machine, and that took a lot of the real hard work off her. She had always said that ironing was lady's work, but washing was rough, so with the washing machine she felt like she was really living in luxury.

School was a real pleasure to me. First of all, if you were in the first grade, like I was, you got a real hot lunch every day, and the teachers and the kids were pretty nice. It was a mixed colored and white school, like the neighborhood, and all the teachers were white, and though I hate to say so, I always found white teachers nicer to black kids than teachers of the same race. Maybe this didn't happen to other kids, but it sure happened to me. Later, when we moved away from The Other Side of the Hill, I went to an all-black school with black teachers, and it was awful to see the way the teachers' pets were always the lightest kids with the straightest hair.

Fall went into winter, and winter that year was really something. Everything was frozen solid for months and months, and we woke up every morning to a glaring white world and a wind that cut right through you no matter how many clothes you wore. I guess because I was born in Ohio, the cold didn't bother me much, but for the people that had started out in the South it was a real cross to bear. Aunt Mary used to wrap herself in so many sweaters and coats that I couldn't figure out how she managed to swing around on those crutches, but somehow she did. She suffered terrible in the winter, though, 'cause with the work she did her hands was almost always in water and they got chapped real bad, so bad that the skin cracked and bled, and she never really had time for them to heal. Finally, Mama brought her a pair of rubber gloves, and that helped some.

Along about the end of March a thaw set in all of a sudden, and the result was a real bad flood over most of the state. Out where we lived things got pretty bad, 'cause the water pipes under the ground busted. The health authorities were afraid of the typhoid and they sent out word we wasn't to use any water unless we boiled it first. The water in the house stopped altogether, and we had to go to a broken pipe in the street to get any water at all. We were luckier than most because where Mama worked there was a well, so she and John bought a big galvanized can and they brought us water we didn't have to be afraid to use.

From the time of the flood to the end of the school term it was just one thing after the other. First, Janet got the measles and the school said Alice and I had to stay home until we couldn't carry it, and then, just when they let us back in, I got impetigo and I was contagious again. I really missed those hot lunches, and the worst thing was that I had missed so much I was left back, but when I realized that being in the first grade for another year meant another year of hot lunches, I didn't feel so bad. Even though Alice was out as much as I was, she didn't get left back. She was always smart and a real good student, and she even went on to college.

Even though the school was mixed white and colored, and even though some of our neighbors were white, being black just wasn't important. Who knows how long I would have gone on feeling just like everybody else? It might have been a long time, but then something happened that changed it all. Mama decided that when summer came, she, Janet, Alice, and I ought to go down to Georgia to see my brother Verne, and get to know our daddy's parents. I guess it was time for lesson number two in being a black woman.

· 3 ·

It was my first trip anywhere and my first time on a train, and I thought I was going to die from the excitement. Aunt Mary had packed a big lunch for the four of us, and John managed to borrow a car somewhere to drive us to the station, and that by itself was going off in style. He drove, and Mama sat on the front seat beside him, and snatches of their talk kept drifting back to where Janet, Alice, and I were.

"You got no call to be so scared, honey," John was saying. "I grew up in the South, and it ain't all that awful. You knows your place and whitey knows his, and if you mind your business he ain't got no reason to mind it for you."

"Hunh!" sniffed my mama. "If it's all so fine how come you high-tailed it out of there as soon as you was big enough?"

"I already explained that to you," said John reasonably. "I didn't want to spent my life chopping cotton, and I heard if I come up north I could get something better to do."

"You could have been a house servant down there, and that's all you are here! I don't see where it made much difference."

John laughed. "You just nervous about your trip, that's
all. Ain't nothing I say you ain't going to argue with, and
you sure ain't going to believe me about Georgia till you get
there and see for yourself. Right?"

I puzzled over what they were saying. How could Mama
be scared about going to see Verne and my daddy's folks?
It just sounded nice to me, but I figured maybe Alice would
know. I always figured Alice would know everything 'cause
she was older and so smart.

Janet was busy looking out the window, and Alice was just
sitting, listening to the grown folk, so I nudged her.

"How come Mama's scared?" I asked. "What's to be scared
of?" Like I said, Alice didn't like me much, and sometimes
she wouldn't talk to me at all, but the one time I could be sure
she would was if I asked her a question 'cause that gave her a
chance to be a smart ass. When I got older I found out she
answered me wrong a lot of the time, but when I was little,
if Alice said it I believed it.

"The lynching," she said, like what dummy wouldn't know
that? I wasn't about to let her know I didn't know what she
was talking about, so I just nodded my head and shut up. The
word didn't sound too bad to me, and I figured Mama was
just having one of those grown-up tizzies that I never understood anyway.

Just about that time we got to the train station, and the
sight of it drove the whole thing clean out of my head. John
loaded himself down with our stuff and kind of led the way
through the crowd, and Mama kept turning around to be sure
the three of us were following right behind. There were a
lot of kids in the station, many of them white, and I remember
feeling sorry for all of them 'cause they weren't going anywhere, and I was. It was a great feeling.

I suppose the Jim Crow car was the worst car on the train,
but I didn't have anything to compare it to, and to me the
dusty green velour seats and the carpet in the aisle and the
brown woodwork looked unbelievably elegant. The whole
car was jammed with black people getting settled for the
trip, and as John put our stuff up on the overhead shelf I

heard him say teasingly to Mama, "Don't it make you feel better to know you ain't going into bondage alone? There's too many of you to string up, and beating you all would be pretty tiresome."

Mama didn't answer. I don't think she thought it was funny. Looking back, I can imagine how she felt. She'd been born and raised in Ohio, and the South was a place you got away from if you were lucky. Sometimes the black people who came from there told stories that they beefed up a little so they'd look smarter or braver, and some of those stories were plenty scary—and some of them were scary and true.

A black man in a white jacket and a black cap came into the car shouting something I couldn't understand, but I guess John did, 'cause he took Mama in his arms and kissed her good-by. Then he kissed the three of us and told us to be good, and he left. The train gave a big lurch and slowly started to move, and I remember how surprised I was when I looked out the window and saw how high we were off the ground and felt how smooth the wheels ran.

The trip from Cincinnati to Atlanta was overnight, and everybody slept in their seats. Folks had all packed lunches, like we did, and everybody was pretty friendly and talkative, so by the time we had been riding for a couple of hours the whole place looked like a big picnic party. There were lots of kids and babies, and the babies were either getting fed or screaming, and the kids were either eating or running up and down the aisle. Alice, who was always kind of snooty, stayed in her seat and read a book or looked out the window, but Janet and I ran with the rest of the kids and had a great time. It began to get late, and the man with the white jacket came back with some pillows to rent. Lots of people just rolled up their coats and used them for pillows, but Mama got a real one for each of us, and we kind of settled down. All night long I kept waking up when the train whistled, and between the whistle and the click-clacking of the train wheels on the tracks, I don't think I've ever felt so happy. There's something about those train noises that just does something to me, like all the danger in the world is outside and here I am, protected and rushing through the night, safe as a white baby. The diesels don't whistle like that any more, but the wheels still click-clack, and I still get that same feeling on the train.

Early in the morning we got to Atlanta, where we had to take a different train for Athens. Uncle Bill, my daddy's brother, met us at the station, and for the four hours that we had to wait for the other train he showed us around his part of town and then took us to his house for lunch. I got introduced to a lot of cousins I didn't even know I had, and Alice and Janet and I had to be kissed, and we had to be polite all the time 'cause Mama was watching us carefully, and I couldn't wait till it was time to leave.

Finally he piled us all back in his truck and drove us back to the station, and we got on the other train. It was what they call a shuttle train, that just runs between Atlanta and smaller towns around it, and even I could see it was awful. The seats were made out of straw and were broken and dirty, the floor was filthy, and some of the windows were broken. It was getting pretty hot outside, and when that train started to pick up speed, the hot, moist air mixed with soot and ashes blew like crazy through those broken window panes. Finally, the three of us and Mama just sat quiet with our eyes closed, and every once in a while Mama cheered us up by telling us we were almost there. It was only about a four-hour trip, but it was so uncomfortable it seemed like forever until we got there.

When the train pulled into Athens the sun was going down, and the cooling air helped perk us up a little bit. Mama had explained that our other grandpa, who we had never seen, was coming in from the country to fetch us, and we expected to see a shuffling man with a hang-dog look, like the grandpa we had left at home. Were we ever surprised! As we were getting down from the train the handsomest man I had ever seen came up to us, a big smile on his face. He *was* a tall man, but being as little as I was he looked like a giant to me, and he was dressed so fine I couldn't take my eyes off of him. He had on a black suit with a white shirt with a turned-around collar, 'cause he was a minister, the shiniest black shoes I ever saw, and he was carrying a black hat. His face was a kind of rich chocolate brown, and what with the brown face and the black suit, his hair, which was silver-white, made him look like the top of his head was lit up. I think if I had been in Sunday school and I was asked to draw a picture of the Lord, I would have made Him look just like that.

In no time at all Mama had introduced us all around, he had gathered up our belongings, and we were all installed in a wagon pulled by two big black horses. He helped Mama up on the front seat, then climbed up himself, and turned around to look at us.

"Coming from the city like you do, I'll bet none of you ever rode behind a horse before. It's a mite slower than you're used to, but a lot more pleasant. Caesar and Panther here, they're two of the nicest, gentlest animals in the whole country, and tomorrow, when I've got you settled down, you can go down to the barn and get acquainted with them. Now, are you all comfortable? Tell me if you're not, 'cause we got about fifteen miles to go."

"Mr. Wilkins," said my mama, "how come Verne didn't ride along with you to the station? I'm very anxious to see him."

Grandpa looked surprised.

"Why, Betty Jo," he said, "we got a farm. Somebody's got to stay behind to milk and do the other chores, and Verne sure isn't old enough to drive all this distance to fetch you all. You know, in the country, ever'body can't go galivanting off at one time."

He gave a funny, clucking noise with his tongue, and we started to move. After the smooth speed of the train it felt like we were standing still and rocking, but the landscape began to slowly move past. When we got out of Athens we were on a narrow country road with tall pines on both sides, and I lay on my back in the straw and watched the tops of the trees sliding by. Janet fell asleep right away, but Alice and I, being older, stubbornly kept our eyes open. Only babies fell asleep before dark, even if dark was a long time in coming. I kind of dozed most of the trip, but we all woke up when we got to

Watkinsville, which was the village just before you got to
Grandpa's farm. I guess what woke us was the wagon
coming to a stop because, although we were on the main
street, it was almost ten o'clock at night, and there were
hardly any lights, certainly not enough to get us up. We
scrambled to our feet in the straw and peered over the side
to see what was going on, just in time to see Grandpa, who
had climbed down from his seat, take off his hat and talk to
a white man on the sidewalk.

"Now, you know, Joe," the white man was saying, "I
can't promise nothing about those kids if you don't teach
them their place. You know how we all feel about you around
here, and we wouldn't do nothing to hurt you or yours, but
Nigra kids got to be taught how to stay out a trouble, and
just 'cause they're your grandbabies, that don't change nothing."

Grandpa nodded his head. "You're right, you're right, Mr.
Bob. It never would have happened except that Verne comes
from the north and ain't learned our ways as good as he
should."

"Well, Colombus knows our ways, don't he? And he was
just as sassy as Verne."

"I'm really sorry, Mr. Bob, and you can be mighty sure it
won't happen again. Wouldn't have happened today, only I
had to drive into Athens to fetch Verne's mama and her three
girls."

Grandpa motioned in the direction of the wagon, and the
white man took a couple of steps toward us so he could see
us better. Mama, who had been sitting on the wagon bench
like she was carved out of stone, sort of drew back like she
wanted to disappear in the shadows.

"This here's my daughter-in-law, Betty Jo," said Grandpa,
"and the three girls are Alice, Ossie, and Janet. They all
coming to spend the summer with their grandma and me.
Betty Jo, this is Mr. Bob Gurnsey; he owns the general store,
right over there." Grandpa pointed to a dark store front
not far away.

"Nice meeting you, Betty Jo," said the white man. "Hope you have a pleasant summer. Ever been south before?"

So low that I could barely hear her Mama said, "No . . . sir."

"Best place in the world to live, right, Joe? Friendly folks and none of them troubles between races like up north. A place for everybody, and everybody in his place, just like the Lord intended. Be a good lesson for your boy to learn, and he's got just the right granddaddy to learn him. Joe here, he's a mighty respected man around these parts. Ain't a Nigra or a white could say a bad word about him, and there ain't many of either I'd say that about."

Grandpa smiled. "Thank you, Mr. Bob. I appreciate it. Now, if you'll excuse me, I got to be getting these young ones home to bed."

The white man waved a kindly hand. "Sure, sure. I know how it is. Got young ones of my own. You just have a word with them boys, hear?"

"Yes, sir! I surely will."

Grandpa climbed up on the wagon bench, and the white man turned away. When we were moving again, Grandpa said proudly, "That Mr. Bob, he's a real good friend of mine. I've heard that my daddy belonged to his granddaddy, 'way back. Don't know how true it is, 'cause things like records got pretty mixed up during the War between the States."

"You saying your own daddy was a slave?" Mama sounded surprised.

"That's what I'm saying," said Grandpa proudly. "My daddy was a slave and here I am, owning my own farm and minister to a good congregation of respectable folks, trusted by white and black alike. Yes, sir, I'm mighty grateful and proud. You mighty quiet there, Betty Jo. Is something wrong?"

I was shocked to hear what sounded like a muffled sob come from my mama. "This whole place gives me the creeps," she half whispered, half sobbed. "John said wasn't nothing to be scared of, but I'm scared anyhow. I wish I'd a stayed home."

"Whoa, there," said Grandpa to the horses, and they pulled to a stop. He laid the reins in his lap and turned around so he was facing Mama and us both.

"Before we go one step further, I want to tell you something, all of you. Now you listen. I'm going to tell you now, so's I don't have to talk about it at the house, 'cause your grandma gets mad if I do. I don't know what you heard about the South up in Ohio, but I live here and I have lived here all my life and I know what I'm talking about. The South is the only place in this country for a black man to live. There's rules, and if you live by them rules, you got as nice a life as you could want. Sure, lots of folks are poor, but from what I hear, most of the brothers up north ain't exactly millionaires, either. Around these parts, ain't no white man pretending to your face that he likes you when he don't, ain't no colored kid thinking he can grow up to be President when he can't, ain't no decent family man running off and leaving his woman and children to scratch for themselves like some of the men up north do. I'm seventy-three years old and I ain't never had no trouble with any white man that I couldn't handle. You ain't got no call to be scared, none at all. You just do what you're supposed to, and the white man, he'll do what he's supposed to. I've lived like that for a long time and I know what I'm talking about."

He turned to Mama, reached out, and patted her hand. "There, now. You feel better?"

Mama smiled weakly. "I don't feel better yet, but I suppose I will if I try."

"That's all you got to do." Grandpa nodded approvingly. "That's all anybody got to do. Just try as hard as you can and don't leave off trying no matter what. That's all the Lord expects of us, and he'll take care of the rest. Now let's get on home."

We didn't really get to see the farm till next morning 'cause we were all so tired we just fell into bed and slept like dead. I do remember Verne and Grandma coming out to meet us, and there was a lot of crying and laughing and Grandma insisting we must be starved, but it's all kind of blurry. There's nothing blurry about the memory of my waking up the next morning, though. I woke with that great feeling that you have when you open your eyes and know something exciting is going to happen and you can't wait for the day to start.

It must have been very early, because the room wasn't really fully light, but I heard little stirrings outside my window and I could smell bacon cooking, and that was enough for me. Alice and Janet, who were in the same bed as me, didn't even stir when I got up, and I was glad because I wanted to explore by myself and besides, as hungry as I was, I figured on eating everything in sight and not sharing if I could help it. I kind of crept down the hall until I could see into the kitchen, but as quiet as I was I guess Grandma heard me.

"C'mon in the kitchen, whoever you are," she called out. "The food's on."

I would have gone even if she hadn't invited me. The smells that were coming out of that kitchen were pulling me in there.

Grandma was standing over the stove with her back to me, but she looked over her shoulder when I came in.

"Morning, Ossie," she said. "You all washed up yet?"

I shook my head.

"All right," she said. "Here's what you do. First you go out that door there to the privy and attend to yourself. Then, when you're done, you go to the well and wash out your mouth and then you come back in here. I already got the water heating on the stove so's you can wash. You understand?"

I nodded. "Then do I get to eat?" I asked.

Grandma smiled broadly. "You sure do. You hurry, now, and I'll be putting your food on the table."

"If Alice and Janet get up, are you going to tell them what they have to do before you let them eat?"

Grandma laughed. "Don't you worry none. I ain't gonna give your breakfast to nobody but you. You was here first, you get your food first. Now, git!"

By the time I got back to the big kitchen Alice and Janet were coming sleepily through the door, and before Grandma could even open her mouth I was telling them what they had to do before they could eat.

There's a price tag on everything that happens to you in this world, and I guess one of the costs of growing up is that nothing has such sharp edges as it does when you're a kid, good or bad. Maybe it's just as well, though, 'cause maybe you can stand things better when you don't feel every last bit of them. On that farm, that summer, I was still young enough to let all the sights and sounds and smells and tastes and hurts and fears and joys really toss me around, and I still remember the great taste of Grandma's cooking, the green, growing smell of the land all around, the joy of playing where it was pretty, the novelty of feeding hogs, shucking corn, digging peanuts and roasting them over an open fire, bathing in a wooden bucket in the kitchen, and the pride on Sunday of all of us putting on our best clothes and riding into town to the church. I felt, sometimes, like I would bust with that pride, 'cause it was *my* grandpa who got up in that pulpit and gave the sermon and talked direct with the Lord. When the services were over we all stood outside with him while members of the congregation came up, one by one, and told him how good his talk had been and looked at us and made a fuss over us 'cause we were his grandchildren. It was my first time at feeling good over who I was and what I was, and it was a feeling I haven't had too much of since then.

We were a real family that summer—Mama, us three girls, Verne, Grandpa and Grandma, and my cousin Colombus, who was my daddy's brother's oldest son. Colombus lived with Grandpa and Grandma just like Verne did, so Grandpa had somebody to help him with the chores, and it was real nice for the boys 'cause they were close to the same age. They worked hard all day, but after supper, which is early on a farm, they could do what they wanted, and what they wanted to do was play. Sometimes they played with us girls, but most often they went off with boys who lived in Watkinsville, and sometimes Grandpa had a hard time rounding them up at bedtime, but he always managed to find them.

Janet and I, being younger, didn't really care when they

went off without us, but Alice got real mad. She would nag and nag and nag them to take her along, and sometimes they would pretend like they were going to and then just disappear without her, and then she would take out her feelings on us and would end up with Mama getting mad and all three of us going to bed crying. Alice was, and still is, one of those people who, when they want something, never give up trying to get it. So one night late in August, instead of asking the boys could she come along, she just decided to follow behind them without their knowing until they got to town, figuring that once she was there with them they wouldn't bother to send her back.

From what I heard later, I guess this is pretty much the way it happened. The two of them were trudging along the narrow dirt road, talking, when they heard a scream from the bushes right near them. They began to run in the direction of the noise and after pushing aside some underbrush they came on Alice and two white boys who looked to be about fifteen or sixteen. One of the boys was holding Alice down on the ground and the other one was trying to get her pants off, but she was squirming so hard they were both having trouble with her. Verne was only twelve and Colombus thirteen, but they were pretty big for their age and good fighters, and they threw themselves at these two white boys. There was a big scuffle and a lot of hard hitting, and some biting from Alice. Then Verne hit one of the white boys so hard he fell on the ground right behind the other white boy at the same minute Colombus was landing a lucky punch on his nose. He stepped back and fell over his friend and hit his head on a tree trunk, and he just lay there like he was dead.

The other white boy got up from the ground and came over to look at his friend, and Alice and Colombus and Verne were like frozen with fear, and they just stood and watched.

"Billy!" said the white boy. "Open your eyes! Billy!"

But the boy on the ground didn't move.

The other one looked up at Alice and the boys.

"Boy, oh boy!" he said with pleasure. "You niggers have really done it now! I sure enough wouldn't want to be in your shoes. You'll probably all get strung up, and it won't be no loss, neither. Looks like you've killed him."

"We didn't kill him!" cried Verne. "You saw!"

"I didn't see nothing," the white boy said. "I was laying on the ground there. I didn't see nothing but you hitting him."

"We can tell how it happened," said Alice. "There's three us can tell how it happened."

"This here ain't Ohio," said the white boy. "This is Georgia, and in Georgia white men tell the truth and niggers lie. Who you think they gonna believe, you or me?"

Just then Billy groaned and opened his eyes. "What happened?"

He looked up at his friend and then at the three black kids, and hate filled his face. He sat up and grabbed his friend by the arm.

"You keep your mouth shut about this, understand? You ain't never seen no nigger knock me down and you ain't never going to see it. I don't want my daddy or no one else neither knowing about this, and you better not tell. And as for you"—he turned his attention on Alice and the boys— "I'm going to take care of you my own way, and if you say one word about what happened to the dressed-up ape that calls himself a preacher, I'll know and you'll wish you was dead. Now you git out of here and you keep quiet, understand? I ain't telling you when or where I'll git you, but you can bet I will, so you all go home and shiver."

Alice and the boys didn't need a second invitation to get out of there. The three of them sprinted for the road as fast as they could go, but they hadn't gone more than a few steps when they ran smack into Grandpa, who had come looking for them. He didn't waste any words.

"I heard," he said, flatly. "You all come with me and don't none of you say one word, you hear?"

He walked straight to where the white boys stood.

"Evening, gentlemen," he said. "I was coming along the road and I heard you and my kids here playing a game. It ain't rightly the kind of game I like them to play, and I know for a fact, Mr. Billy, your daddy wouldn't like it none neither, so I guess it would be better if we didn't tell him about it. Course, if something unpleasant happens to any of my kin, I guess it would be my duty to tell him, but I sure hope I don't have to. Your daddy's got a right powerful temper when he's angered."

Alice told me later she expected the white boys to beat Grandpa up, but nothing like that happened. They just looked at him sullenly and then turned around and walked away.

"Now," said Grandpa, "let's get on home. Your mama will be worrying." Alice said he never said another word all the way home, and since none of them were about to say anything, it was a very silent walk. It was only when they got to the front yard that Grandpa broke the silence.

"You ain't hurt none, are you?" he asked Alice.

She shook her head.

"Well, then," said Grandpa, "there's no harm done and no need to tell your mama and your grandma anything at all. You all know I hold with truth-telling and honesty, but sometimes, like now, it's better just to not stir up a lotta excitement for nothing. I think you all should just go in the house and go to bed."

"Grandpa?" asked Alice. "Would that Mr. Billy's father really be so mad at him?"

Grandpa nodded. "He would, but it would be a private mad. His public mad would have to be at the boys here, and that could be mighty unpleasant for everybody."

"But we didn't do nothing bad—they did. In school the teacher always says if you haven't done nothing to be ashamed of, then you should stand right up and look the world square in the eye and put the blame right where it belongs," Alice protested.

"Maybe someday," said Grandpa wistfully, "we going to have a world where you can do just that, but in the meantime we got to live in the world we got, and in this world it's enough to know you doing the best you can. A man can respect himself when he knows that. What everybody else thinks counts some, but what you think about *you*, that's what really matters. Besides, you wasn't all blameless. You run off tonight and you got yourself and the boys in a heap of trouble. Like I was telling you that first night you come here, if you don't look for trouble, you won't find it. Now go to bed."

Alice took Grandpa's advice and didn't tell Mama, but she couldn't resist telling me. By the next morning she had gotten over her scare and felt like a heroine, and she just had to have somebody to show off to. I got pretty sick of listening to how she almost got raped, particularly since I didn't know what "raped" meant. She said I was too young to tell but I don't think she was sure of what it meant either. I didn't puzzle over it long, though. I just decided it meant getting your pants stolen.

Those white boys never did cause any trouble for Verne and Colombus, and Grandpa looked even bigger to me than he had before. When I got older it kind of seemed to me that because Grandpa knew he was a man, he didn't have to prove it by throwing his weight around, so he faced the world and really looked at it and then picked his way through the best way for him and his.

Funny, isn't it? I got lesson two in being a black woman from Grandpa, who was really a man.

· 4 ·

In June, with school just out and the summer stretching ahead like a long day in an amusement park, you hope it will never end, but by August you're tired of trying to figure out what to do next and you kind of start wishing that it was time for teachers and lessons and cold mornings when getting up was proof that you were brave. I seem to remember things by the way they smelled, and the difference between June and August is that June smells like new grass and flowers and lovely warm air, and August like dust and heat.

Alice's big moment began to fade into the past enough for her to stop telling me about it over and over, and with that excitement gone things began to get dull. You know how it is—the first time you feed the hogs you don't see it as work 'cause it's new, but the twentieth time it's something you'd rather not do but you have to. With kids, when this kind of feeling sets in you have nothing but fights, and that's what started to happen between all of us. The slightest little thing could start a ruckus, and one or the other of us was always running to Mama or Grandma to complain about what somebody else was doing to us. Mama and Grandma took it for a while, and then *they* started getting riled over *our* being riled, and things were getting pretty unpleasant. Grandpa didn't seem to pay any mind to all of it, but he must have heard, and I remember expecting him to blow up and really paddle us, but he never did. He had this wonderful way of not letting anything bother him unless it was really worth getting bothered about, which is great for the person who has it, but very trying for others that he lives with. I remember hearing Grandma urging him to crack down on us because we were gettting out of hand, and I remember how mad she got when he just smiled and said, "The difference between young ones and grown-ups is that young ones are still free enough to act like they feel. Be glad they can do it. They got enough years when they're gonna have to pretend."

"That's well enough for you to say," sniffed Grandma. "You ain't listening to them fight all day. Betty Jo and I are just about drove out of our minds."

"Rise above it," counseled Grandpa. "Just rise above it. Ain't nothing you can't rise above if you've a mind to."

"Ain't nothing *you* can't rise above, you mean. I don't hold with all this rising. There are times when instead of rising you should come down heavy. Them kids need to be put down some, and they need to be put down by you."

"How come you can't do it?" asked Grandpa.

" 'Cause they don't pay no mind to their mama or me, that's why."

"Well, now," said Grandpa seriously, "do you think that might be because you both come down on them heavy for every little thing? Maybe they think you're like the boy who cried wolf. They just don't believe you."

From the look on Grandma's face, I think if she had been a swearing woman she would have cussed him out right then and there. Instead, she just turned her back on him so she didn't have to see the twinkle in his eye. As I say, he was a mighty good man, and sometimes they're the hardest kind to live with and, as we kids found out not long after, they're the most frightening when they do finally rise up in righteous wrath.

It all started late one afternoon. Supper was over, the chores were done, Mama and Grandma were sitting on the porch getting a breath of air, and Grandpa had gone off to visit a sick member of his congregation. Us five kids were hanging around down at the barn, tired of nothing to do, tired of each other, tired of stealing watermelon from the watermelon patch, and ready for anything. Alice, as usual, was lugging a book, but she wasn't really reading it, just turning pages.

Verne and Colombus had drawn a line in the dirt with a stick and were trying to see who could back up the furthest and clear the line when he jumped toward it. The line was pretty near where Alice was sitting with her book, and every time they made a jump they almost landed on her, but Alice being Alice and the boys being boys, nobody gave an inch. They jumped a few more times and just missed her, but then Colombus gave out with his strongest effort and landed right in front of her, lost his balance, knocked the book out of her hand, and sent her and himself sprawling. Alice picked herself up off the ground swinging and hit Colombus as hard as she could. Her open hand caught him across the ear and the tears came to his eyes, probably from pain more than anything else, but Verne didn't care.

"Hey, Alice!" he said with relish. "Look what you done! You made the big boy cry."

"I ain't crying," protested Colombus, "and nobody who don't want to cry himself better say so."

"You are too crying," chimed in Alice. "That there's water in your eyes. Anybody can see that."

Janet and I felt left out, so we started in too.

"Colombus is crying, Colombus is a baby! Look at the baby still sucking on his mama's titty!"

I looked at Colombus, expecting to see him attack us all. Instead, a kind of sneaky look came into his eyes, and ignoring us three girls he looked right at Verne and said in a low tone, "I slept with your mama last night."

Verne, who had been expecting a physical attack, was completely taken by surprise. He just kind of stood there with his mouth hanging open, waving his balled-up fists, hitting air.

Alice, who was much quicker on the uptake, planted herself in front of Colombus. "You're a liar!"

Like he was clearing flies out of the air, Colombus brushed her away. "You ain't no boy," he said with contempt. "This here's for boys."

Verne, challenged, finally reacted. "You're a liar . . . and a prick!"

We gasped. That was a pretty bad word, and Mama didn't allow words like that. It didn't seem to faze Colombus, though. He just kept his eyes on Verne's face.

"I slept with your mama last night," he repeated, "and I got her drawers in my pocket."

A funny, blank look came over Verne's face, like he had raised his hand to it and wiped it clean of emotion.

"You're a motherfucker," he said flatly.

"Your mama's one."

The three of us girls stood there frozen with horror, looking from Verne to Colombus and back again, tingling with shock and wicked anticipation over what they would say next. We had never heard so many dirty things in our whole life, and it was great.

"You're a son of a bitch," Verne snapped.

"I seen your mama with no clothes on." Colombus sounded triumphant, like he had played his trump card.

Verne didn't answer. He seemed to be reaching some place inside himself, looking for the worst thing he could think of to say.

"All the things you're saying about my mama ain't true. You just know about these things 'cause you do them with *your* mama. You're a motherfuckin' nigger!"

"Silence!"

The rich, full, angry voice seemed to fill the whole yard. It was like the voice of the Lord come to wreak his punishment on the sinners. We all started to shake and instinctively drew closer to each other as Grandpa descended on us from behind the barn. We had spent almost three months with him, and I thought I knew every way he could look, but I had never seen him like this before. He seemed to have gotten even taller, and his usually kind face had such a look of rage and disgust that he didn't even look familiar, and his voice was roughened and loud, like the voice of doom. He planted himself in front of us and just glared. Struck dumb with fear, we stared back. The minute that we stood like that seemed to go on forever, and I had a wild thought that maybe the Lord had punished us by turning us all to stone, but then, so suddenly that we all jumped, Grandpa raised his arm and pointed his finger at Colombus.

"You, boy, you're the oldest. You got some reason to give me for what I just heard?"

Involuntarily, Colombus took one step back.

"Don't step back!" Grandpa roared. "Step up! Step up and give me and the Lord a reason for what you was doing and saying!"

Colombus, looking like he was going to die right on the spot, did as he was told.

"We was just playing a game," he said, so low that I was surprised Grandpa heard him. I guess I looked at him with a kind of awe. The trouble we were in was bad enough, without lying to Grandpa.

"It was just a game," he repeated, as though saying it twice would make it so.

Grandpa turned his terrible stare on Verne. "Is that true? Were you playing a game, like Colombus says?"

Verne darted a glance at Colombus. He seemed to be trying to figure out whether he was in more trouble lying or not lying.

"He didn't know it was a game," Colombus said flatly. "I did, but he didn't. He was just doing it cause I ragged him into it."

With surprise, I realized that Colombus wasn't lying after all, or at least he sure didn't sound like he was. I guess Grandpa must have felt the same way.

"That ain't like no game I ever heard of. Where'd you learn it? What's the name of it?"

"Neely, over to Watsonville, told me about it. It's called 'doin' the dozen,' and I ain't never played it before, honest! I just wanted to try it once, but I won't do it again, honest I won't! Wasn't much fun, anyway."

Grandpa started looking more like I was used to.

"C'mon," he said. "Let's all go over here to the haystack and set. We got things to talk about."

Meekly, we did as we were told. Some of the fear had gone out of us, but Grandpa still looked pretty serious, and we knew we weren't cleansed yet.

"When I was coming up," Grandpa said, "I heard about that game, only I heard about it the way it used to be, and I heard how it started and why it started. It was a game slaves used to play, only they wasn't just playing for fun. They was playing to teach themselves and their sons how to stay alive. The whole idea was to learn to take whatever the master said to you without answering back or hitting him, 'cause that was the way a slave had to be, so's he could go on living. It maybe was a bad game, but it was necessary. It ain't necessary now. Now it's like making a slave out of yourself when you ain't one, and it's also an offense to the Lord. Words like I just heard you all use and the way you was using them, that's as surely an offense to the Lord as if you had killed somebody, 'cause you are killing somebody and the somebody's you. Mostly all a person's got in this world is his own self-respect, and a man that respects himself don't disrespect other people. You all understand what I'm saying?"

He let his eyes travel to our faces, one by one, and when he looked straight at me I felt he could see down inside me to where all the bad things were. I guess he must have satisfied himself that we all knew what he meant, and I was just beginning to feel the relief that comes when the worst is over, when he said in a nice, pleasant voice, "Colombus, go fetch me my paddle."

Colombus looked startled. I guess he had felt like I did, relieved.

"Your paddle?" he said stupidly. "How come you want your paddle?"

"Never mind how come," said Grandpa, still in the same pleasant way. "Just git it."

"You gonna paddle the boys?" asked Alice hopefully.

Grandpa nodded. "And the girls, too," he said.

"We didn't do nothing," Alice protested. "We was just standing there, and besides Colombus started the whole thing 'cause he jumped on me. I was just reading my book, and he jumped on me."

"I know what you did and didn't do," said Grandpa. "I know what you heard and what you saw, too, and I don't want you to forget it or what I said about it. Some day you gonna have boys of your own, and when that day comes you got a heavy load resting on you to bring up them boys to have self-respect. That's a trick for any mama, and for a black mama it's even trickier, and you gonna need all the help you can get, so I'm gonna help you. Every time you hear a black man or woman or child treat themselves or anybody else like they was still slaves, you gonna remember how that paddle felt on your backside and you gonna remember what I said."

"I'll remember what you said, Grandpa," I offered. "I'll remember without no paddling to call it to mind."

Grandpa looked at me and smiled. "That's what you think now, Ossie, but things don't work out that way. Seems like people just naturally remember things better when they hurt a little."

"Well, *I* won't!" Alice shrieked, stamping her foot in the dirt. "It ain't fair that Ossie and Janet and me should get paddled when we didn't do nothing! If you get smacked when you don't do nothing and you're good, then you might as well quit all the worrying and be bad! I'm going to tell Mama what you're doing!"

Grandpa didn't try to stop her. He just sat where he was, looking kind of serious, with the three of us watching him to see what would happen next.

All three of them came back at the same time, Colombus carrying the stick that Grandpa called his paddle, Alice crying and looking defiant and scared all at the same time, and Mama with her lips set and her eyes scurrying from one to the other of us.

Grandpa stood up. "Betty Jo," he said, "I been aiming to

teach the young ones the way I was taught and the way I set
store by. I'll go on teaching Colombus, 'cause his mama and
daddy ain't here and I'm his grandpa, but you *are* here and you
got first say on what happens to your children. If you don't
want me to paddle them, why all you got to do is say so."

Mama looked at us, and we looked back, trying to look as
pitiful as we could. She seemed to think for a minute, but then
she reached out and took the stick from Colombus and handed
it to Grandpa. Our hearts sank.

"I don't see where a paddling will hurt them none," she
said, "as long as they know what it's for."

Grandpa nodded. "I just finished telling them that. They
know what it's for."

Mama shook her head. "Alice told me what you said, and
maybe you think that's what it's for, but it ain't."

"I don't rightly follow you," said Grandpa, with surprise.
"What you mean?"

"I mean you ain't paddling them 'cause they was bad, you're
paddling them 'cause they're black, and they might as well get
to know it right now. It's like your Mr. Bob said that first
night we come here—'Nigra kids got to be taught to stay
outa trouble'; ain't that what he said? I was pretty scared that
night and I wanted to go home, but I been doing some thinking, sitting here this summer, and I can see it ain't any different
here than anyplace else; it's just more out in the open. You
want your black boy to stay out of trouble, you teach him his
place when he's young. That white man was giving good advice, so you just go on and paddle. Only thing is, maybe they
shouldn't use bad words, but that 'doin' the dozen'—there's
nothing wrong with that game. My brothers used to play it
back in Cincinnati and they always said it taught them to hold
their temper."

Grandpa laid down the stick. He seemed to be more upset
by what Mama said than he was by what we did.

"I hate to hear anyone say what you just said, Betty Jo.
That's just plain bitterness, and bitterness comes from fighting
the will of the Lord and there ain't no peace, no, nor wisdom
neither, from doing that. Black is the color of your skin, black

isn't you. You're you, and you got an immortal soul that you're gonna have to account for on the Day, and that immortal soul ain't black or white. I wouldn't teach no different to a white boy, 'cause I'm just teaching truth and ain't no color invented yet that can change the truth."

Mama didn't answer, but I could see she didn't pay no mind. It took a lot more than words to ever convince Mama of anything, and when the words were about being black, I don't think anyone could change her mind. She just stood there and watched Grandpa paddle us, one by one. The only one that screamed and carried on was Alice, and she was just being fractious, because I'm sure Grandpa didn't hit her any harder than he hit me, and the way he hit me there wasn't no need to cry.

I don't know if the other kids remembered that day very long, but it sure made an impression on me, and it wasn't the paddling I remembered, it was what Grandpa said about self-respect. In the years after I came up, I never stopped puzzling over how you could live in this world, do the things necessity made you do, and respect yourself, too. You got to admit that's a hard question, and I wish I had been old enough to ask it of Grandpa, but by the time I was, he wasn't in this world any more.

Even though we didn't leave the farm for a couple of weeks after that day, I sort of look on that scene in the yard as the end of the summer in Georgia. Alice started talking about getting back to school, and I started remembering those hot lunches, and Mama was lonely for John, and Janet was starting to school with Alice and me, so we all had something to look forward to . . . and that's a nice feeling.

· 5 ·

John met us at the Cincinnati station with welcome in his eyes and big news on his lips. While we'd been in Georgia, he had found us a house in Camp Dennison, which was a real step up for us. It was a suburb, almost out in the country, and by living there we could go to the little Camp Dennison school, which had mostly white kids and was so small that different grades shared the same room. He had done all the moving while we were away, and all we had to do now was let him take us home to our new house. Alice, Janet, and I, being kids, were all excited, and Mama, being Mama, was suspicious.

"How come you didn't write me what was in your mind?" she asked John as we rode along in the truck.

John grinned. "'Cause I wanted to see your face when I told you."

"I've heard that neighborhood's very high," Mama said. "You come into money or something?"

"The house ain't costing one penny more than Terrace Park. Got me a bargain."

"I'll bet it ain't got but one bedroom. Couldn't have, if it costs the same as Terrace Park," Mama insisted.

"We got three sleeping rooms," said John. "Course, we ain't got no inside plumbing, but we got us a real little farm, with hogs and chickens, and we can have us our own eggs and butter and cream."

"A farm!" cried Mama. "What for we need a farm? And whose gonna do the farming while you and I are at work? Did you stop to think of that?"

John didn't turn a hair. "The girls had a whole summer to learn farming."

Mama glared at him. "They only little girls. They can't run no farm."

"They can with Aunt Mary and Robbie to help."

"How come you didn't say that before?" demanded Mama. "You didn't tell me Aunt Mary and Robbie was going to be there, too. I think you just looking to rile me."

"Didn't I tell you that?" asked John with a wicked grin. "I sure thought I did. That's one of the reasons I went looking in Camp Dennison. Aunt Mary didn't want Robbie working in that bar any longer than he had to, and living in the country he can earn his keep by doing chores for the neighbors and helping around our place, too. And the girls can learn hog slopping and chicken raising and how to catch a husband, all at the same time."

"I don't know how come I let you get me all het up," said Mama with a smile. "I never remember you just like to fun with me."

John patted her shoulder. "You just keep on getting het up. I like you that way. Think you can stay het up till tonight?"

Before Mama could answer, we turned off onto the narrow dirt road that led to our new house. I guess it wasn't much to look at, but after the shacks in Georgia it looked like a palace, with an upstairs and a downstairs and shutters on the white-clapboard sides. There was a front yard and two big oak trees with leaves that were just beginning to turn, and the whole place had a real homey look . . . and in the next few years it turned out to be the best and the last home I was to have for a long time.

They're important years, the ones from eight to twelve, and

for a girl, you start on them a child and end on them a woman.
They were hard-working years for us all, but you don't mind
work when you're happy. Mama and John went back to living
in on their job and even getting to go to Florida every winter
when the people they worked for took them along to their
winter home, but we didn't mind 'cause Aunt Mary and
Robbie were family, too. We went to school and, as usual,
Janet and I just got by, but Alice was always at the head of
the class. The teachers were white and so were most of the
kids, but it didn't matter, because nobody made it matter, and
in those years of my life the color of my skin didn't even en-
ter my mind. Just like John had said, that first day on the
way from the station, we slopped hogs, raised chickens,
gathered eggs, churned butter, learned to cook and to clean,
went to school, and grew up. The growing up happened so
gradually that I didn't think about it at all until the day that
Alice got her first monthly, and from that time on I didn't
think about anything else. You'd have thought she invented
the whole thing, she was so proud and put on such airs. She
started talking about me as "that child" and calling Janet "the
baby," and you can imagine how much Janet and I liked that,
and then, to top it all off, she got a boyfriend. His name was
Roy, and I suppose he was a nice enough boy, but I figured
if he liked Alice, there must be something wrong with him.
They went to great lengths to hide from me when school was
out so they could walk home alone together, and I used to let
them think I wasn't around, but I really was, hiding and spy-
ing. I was dying to see them do something they shouldn't
so's I could get even with Alice for all her airs, but the most
I ever saw them do was kiss, and even that was on the cheek.
That was one of the most aggravating things about Alice. She
never did anything wrong.

The Second World War had started, but in Camp Dennison
it all seemed very far away. We gathered together all the tin
cans we could find and saved them up for John to take to
town, and the ladies like Aunt Mary went and learned first
aid, and once in a while you'd see a young man from around
the neighborhood wearing a uniform, but other than that

things went on like before. There must have been some important battles in 1943, but for me it was the year I stopped having to let Alice call me "little girl," and it was the year I learned the facts of life, not by hearing them but by doing them.

When you live on a farm you learn about life pretty early, and if Alice hadn't been the smart ass she was I would probably have just accepted the fact that humans are animals too, but she wouldn't have it that way. She was always telling me that she knew things I didn't know and couldn't till I was older, and of course I was itching with curiosity, so when I was offered a chance to find out for myself, I didn't even think twice about accepting.

It was after school on a warm October afternoon. Most of the kids had already left the school yard to walk home, but my teacher had made me stay late to do over a paper loaded with spelling mistakes, so by the time I was ready to go home the grounds were empty, except for a couple of real little kids and a boy from my class named Albert. He was kind of just hanging around, and it never occurred to me that he was waiting for me until he fell in next to me as I left. He just walked along, not saying anything, until we got out where the corn fields were.

"You want me to walk steady with you, every day?"

I stopped dead in my tracks. Albert had never singled me out to talk to, he hadn't chosen me in any of the games we played at school, he hadn't even ever written me a secret note —and here he was offering to walk steady with me! A feeling of triumph came over me. Alice wasn't the only one with a boyfriend. Now I had one, too. I looked at him and nodded.

"Okay," I said. "I don't mind."

He stuck out his hand.

"C'mon," he said. "Let's go this way."

I looked where he was pointing. It wasn't the road home, but instead a little scraggly path that led deep into the harvested patch of corn. From following Alice, I knew she and Roy never went that way, so I just naturally wanted to go. I took his hand and sort of followed him. He walked like he knew where he was going, like he'd been there before. Silently we went on till we were out of sight of the road and finally came to a little clearing where somebody had taken a pile of corn husks and mixed them with hay and made a little mound. Albert let go of my hand and took off his shirt and laid it on the mound and then sat down and looked up at me, like he was waiting for something.

"What you doing?" I asked. "We ain't never gonna get home with you sitting down."

He patted a place next to him. "Come sit with me a spell. Ain't hardly four yet. If we gonna walk steady we gotta sit steady, too."

I considered. Alice didn't sit steady, but then maybe Albert knew more about it than Roy did. Anything I could learn that Alice didn't know about was great with me. I sat.

"You ever walk out with anybody before?" Albert asked.

I shook my head.

"Then I'll tell you how to do it."

He leaned over and began to unbutton my blouse, very slowly, looking into my face all the while. When he got all the buttons open he put his hand on my new little breast that I was so proud of, and a feeling started in my legs like nothing I'd ever felt before. I forgot about Alice then and there. There was nobody in the world but me and Albert's hand. I guess when he saw that I wasn't going to cry or run away he was relieved. He stopped looking into my face and instead moved toward me and put his other hand up under my skirt, resting his fingers on the top of my thigh and tapping them a little, and every time he tapped I jumped.

"You gonna let me slide it in?" he asked, almost in a whisper.

Mutely, I nodded. I wasn't sure what came next, but whatever it was, I wanted it, like I had never wanted anything in my life. I laid back, and closed my eyes, ready for anything, not thinking, not knowing, just feeling. I was dimly aware that Albert was fiddling with my underpants and I felt the cool air on my body when he got them off, and then even that was drowned in the feeling of his body covering mine. He raised himself up and pushed my legs apart and entered me, not sliding, like he had said, but pushing and shoving and hurting until all the feelings came together and I couldn't separate the pain from the pleasure. He seemed to be in the grip of some strange spell, moving and moaning and snorting, and just when I began to feel like the pain was getting too bad, he collapsed and fell on me, gasping like he was choking and just laying there. I waited a minute to see what would happen next, but nothing did, and with disappointment I realized it was over. It seemed to me there should be more, somehow, and I was kind of let down.

Albert pulled himself off of me, not meeting my eyes, and pretended he was busy straightening his clothes. With a start I realized I was laying there all uncovered and when I realized that, all the things I had heard about bad girls and the things that happened to them because they were evil washed over me with such force I thought I was drowning in guilt. Frantically trying to pull my pants up and my skirt down at the same time, I scrambled to my feet and started to run blindly, anywhere, any place, just to put as much distance as I could between me and Albert and the place where I had let the devil take over my soul. I ran until every breath I took burned like fire, until my heart thumped so loud it was the only sound I could hear, until just the effort to put one foot in front of the other took up my mind and I couldn't think and I couldn't feel. I got myself good and lost, and the fall day was fading into night when finally, tired out, sobbing, dirty from falling down and soiled from what I had done, I crept into our front yard.

Aunt Mary was standing out on the front porch, peering into the dusk. When she saw me she started down the steps toward me.

"Ossie, where you been? I been looking and Robbie's been looking and we're both about to drop with worrying."

As she spoke she came closer and closer, until finally she could see me and the state of my clothes. She reached out and took me by the shoulder and pulled me toward her.

"Child, what happened to you? You been fighting?"

Miserably, I nodded. I knew Aunt Mary wouldn't take kindly to my fighting, but it was sure better to admit to fighting than to what I had been doing.

She looked disappointed. "I thought you was through with fighting. You sure should be, a big girl like you. Alice don't fight none, any more, and you're always wanting to be as grown up as she is. My, my, look at your dress. It's all torn and dirty and even your underpants. . ."

She had lifted my dress and was looking down at what I, in my panic, hadn't even noticed, large spots of what could only be blood. That's when I really got scared. I thought I was dying, and I started to cry in great gasping sobs, sure that the Lord was punishing me for sinning and very sorry for myself 'cause I was too young to die.

"You stop that squalling!" Aunt Mary's voice was like a knife. "You stop that squalling and come into the house and don't you say one word to nobody until I get a chance to talk to you. Understand? You jest fell down, that's all they got to know. Now you remember, and you do as I say or I'll really tan your hide. Now git in there and get cleaned up for supper."

I think that was the longest meal I ever sat through. Luckily for me, Alice had won first prize in the school composition contest and she had just found out about it that afternoon, so she was so prideful and full of herself that no one had a chance to get a word in, even if they had wanted to. Aunt Mary went through the business of getting supper, tight-mouthed and thin-lipped, and as soon as it was over she set Alice and Janet to cleaning up the dishes, sent Robbie on an errand, and pulled me into her room and shut the door. She sat down on the edge of her bed and pushed me down next to her.

"Now," she said, "you tell me what happened to you today."

I wanted to answer her, I really did, but no words would come. All during supper my throat had been closed tight with dread, dread of something I couldn't even imagine. I knew it wasn't Aunt Mary, because no matter how disappointed she might be in me or how mad she might get, I knew that she loved me, and in time we'd be comfortable together again. It wasn't really fear of anything mortal, or at least that's the way it seemed to me. It was just a cold, bad, painful feeling that had started when I ran away from Albert, a feeling like the Lord had judged me and found me wanting, and I could never be washed clean again. It felt awful, and I remember thinking that I couldn't stand it if it didn't go away soon. It's a good thing I didn't know then how long it was going to last.

Aunt Mary took ahold of my shoulder and pushed me back and forth.

"Ossie," she said, "I'm talking to you and you gotta talk to me. There ain't nothing you done or nothing you ever gonna do you can't tell me, 'cause I'll try to understand, but if you don't tell me, I ain't gonna understand *that*. Was you with a boy today?"

I nodded, my eyes glued to her face, waiting to see the disgust I was sure she would feel, but her expression didn't change at all, that I could see. She just looked serious, like she had all along.

"Did he make you, or did you want to?"

"I wanted to," I whispered. The tears that I had been trying to hide brimmed over and ran single file down my cheeks. They tickled and I brushed them away, but more kept taking their place.

Aunt Mary didn't say anything for a long time. She seemed to be turning things over in her mind, and I was sure that no matter how kind she might be, the fact that I had done what I did because I *wanted* to would be more than even she could accept. Then she reached out and put her arm around me and drew me to her.

"You ain't the first and you won't be the last," she said. "It don't make much sense that the Lord made women loving and then said it was wrong if it ain't your husband, but that's what He did say, and that's what we all gotta learn. To start with, we gotta learn the difference between loving and lusting. You too young for loving, but lusting starts early, like it done with you today."

"At the beginning," I said slowly, "I don't think I was lusting. I just wanted to do it so's I could show Alice I wasn't a little girl any more. The lusting came later."

For a minute, Aunt Mary looked like she was struggling not to laugh, but then she said seriously, "That was pride, sinful pride you was feeling, and that's one of the faces of the devil, and you looked at the devil's face and he led you into sinning some more. Maybe it's a good thing that it happened while you're still so young. You think you'd know the devil next time you see him?"

I said yes, and I really meant it, but I didn't know then how many faces the devil could wear, or that he lived inside of me, ready to take over any time I forgot to watch out for him. It wasn't much more than three hours later, lying in my bed and thinking over what happened to me that day, that I found myself filled again with the painful pleasure that first came to me when Albert touched me, and when I finally fell asleep it was in the middle of the part where he was reaching under my skirt to start his fingers tapping on my thigh. If Grandpa had done a sermon about me, he would have said that I had bitten the apple of knowledge and been expelled from the garden of innocence, and he would have been right, because from that time on I've wandered where the fruit was lush but poisoned, and I've eaten my fill, getting a little sicker with each bite, but unable to stop.

· 6 ·

My experience with albert in the corn field didn't lead
to my walking out with him, after all, although he really
wanted to. It was my doing, not his, and at the same time I
didn't understand it. All I knew was that I couldn't stand to be
around him. If he walked up to me, I walked away; if he sat
next to me, I moved my seat; if he waited for me after school,
I ducked and ran. I took to keeping away from almost every-
one, because no matter how hard I tried I couldn't keep my
eyes and mind off boys, and I figured the devil was trying to
get his hands on me again. I had to fight him off, so I fought
the only way I knew, by running away. At first the other
kids teased me, then they decided I was crazy, and finally they
just lost interest and left me alone.

Out of sheer loneliness, I started trying to read better, and
since the only book Aunt Mary kept in the house was the Bible,
that was what I read. At first I had terrible trouble understanding the words, but bit by bit, with Aunt Mary as a kind
of interpreter, the book began to make sense to me and I dis-
covered, to my surprise, that it was interesting, something
Aunt Mary had tried to tell me for a long time. My new

interest in it started in September, and by the end of December I felt a personal involvement with John the Baptist, with Barabbas, and, above all, with Jesus.

Graduation time was coming close, and Aunt Mary and Alice decided I could wear Alice's graduation dress, with just a little fixing over. I would have liked a new dress of my own, but Aunt Mary said it was a sin not to use what we had, so I stopped looking longingly into store windows and told myself I was a little closer to the angels. I really tried with all my might to believe that I was learning to put the devil behind me, but like a sore tooth, my aching conscience throbbed on and on, until it forced me to try for comfort from Alice.

I waited until I could find a time to bring up what was on my mind without her being aware of how much it meant to me, but as usual with her, I couldn't fool her.

"Alice," I asked in a shaky little voice, "do you know much about lusting?"

Alice looked up at me from the floor, where she was pinning up the hem in her old and my new graduation dress.

"What kind of a stupid question is that?" she demanded.

"What . . ." I forced myself to stumble on, "what I mean is, do you . . . I mean, have you . . ."

"If you're trying to ask me if I've ever done it, the answer is no. You think I'm some kind of idiot?" She looked up at me sharply. "Have you?"

I could have kicked myself for having started the whole thing, and I didn't know what to say. I would have given anything to say no as firmly as she had, to lie and have her believe me, but I knew it wouldn't work. I just couldn't bring myself to say yes either, so I didn't answer.

"Okay," she said, tossing her head, "you don't have to tell me. I can guess. Man, you're even dumber than I thought you were. I thought you knew about sex."

"I do!" I protested. "I know all about it."

"Like hell you do!" she snorted. "Why, you don't even know how to use it."

"Use it?" I repeated feebly.

"That's what I said. Use it. If you don't, you'll end up like all the rest of the dumb black girls, with a houseful of kids and no man to take care of them. Sex is great, the greatest thing you got going for you, but you gotta know how to play it smart. You think you're the only one lusting? Everybody does."

I felt a great surge of relief. At least it wasn't only me.

"Boys lust even more than girls," Alice was saying. "That's what makes it so crazy. When a boy lusts after you, that's when you can get him to do what you want. You've got to make them feel you're going to let them, and then when they're so horny they can't see straight, you kind of pull back and whisper you're afraid. Then, when they say there ain't nothing to be afraid of, you start talking about how you'd love to have a charm bracelet, or a new scarf, or see a certain movie, and they'll fall all over themselves getting you what you want, 'cause they figure once you've got what *you* want, you'll give them what *they* want. It's lots of fun."

She looked so smug I wanted to hit her, but I knew if I did, she'd stick the whole paper of pins in my leg. Even though she was finished second-year high and acted so grown up and uppity, she was as mean as ever, and I was still afraid of her, but I was awed by her, too, 'cause she was so smart in school and was even planning to go on to college. She was really something. She wanted nice clothes, so she went out and got a job and spent a lot of the money she earned on fixing herself up to look good, but she always put a little by for when she was ready for college, and her grades were always the highest in her class. I could never be the student Alice was or the talker Alice was, and here she was telling me something else I could never be—the smart female Alice was.

Instead of hitting her, I just stood crooked so she had to do the whole hem over and really made her mad, but luckily Mama came in just then, and we were both so glad to see her that the whole thing was forgotten.

Mama had come for my graduation. I knew she was coming and I had worried some about seeing her now that I was a sinner, but I forgot to be afraid when I saw her face and heard her voice. I just felt glad all over. We didn't get to see

Mama or John very often, 'cause the family they worked for had taken to doing a lot of traveling, and they were so rich that when they went down to Florida or anywhere they took Mama and John along to do for them.

It turned out Alice didn't have to do the hem on her old dress after all, because Mama had brought me a graduation dress of my own, or at least almost my own. The daughter of the people she worked for had only worn the dress once when she gave it to Mama for me, and that was close enough to new for me. It fit me perfectly, and I must say I really enjoyed the graduation more because I knew I had the nicest dress of any of the girls.

Graduation wasn't really all that much; it was only a little class from a little school, but after it was over Aunt Mary made a special dinner, and the family said they were proud of me, and I felt pretty good.

"What with Alice planning to go to college and Ossie going into high, you really gonna have an educated family," Aunt Mary said to Mama as she passed the roast around.

Mama nodded. "That's all fine," she said, "and I'm proud of them, but there's other things they got to learn, too. Reading and knowing how to write a good sentence are nice, but if a girl has to earn enough to buy food, she can't do it with them tools, leastwise not a black girl."

"Oh, Mama!" Alice got her fighting look on. "You sound like you're a hundred years old. It's on account of people thinking like you that all the colored end up doing housework. There's no reason any more for thinking that way. This isn't slavery; things have changed and they're gonna change still more. *I'm* not going to spend my life working in some white kitchen!"

"How come you're doing it now?" Mama asked sweetly.

Alice glared. "You know how come I'm doing it now. I'm not even out of high yet, and I'm not old enough to get a regular job in an office or something like that."

Mama nodded, with her "I told you so" air. "That's just what I was saying. When a black girl needs money she can always get it if she knows how to cook and clean and wash and iron."

"When they're too young to do anything else, lots of white boys deliver newspapers. That don't mean they're never going to do anything else, does it? When they grow up and they get educated, they find regular jobs, and so can we."

"You musta read that in some of those books you're always toting. You wait till you get out there and try to get one of those 'regular' jobs, and then come and tell me what colored ought to be doing."

"I *sure* will," Alice flared. "By the time I go looking for a job I won't be like the rest of the dumb colored. I'll have me a college degree and I won't have to take any crap from anybody!"

"You just watch the way you talk," Mama ordered sternly. "Don't do no good to have a college degree if you gonna talk like a no-account. Anyway, Ossie here ain't planning to go to college, so she needs to know how to work in a white kitchen, and I got her a job."

I was dumb-struck. I was scared enough about going to the big high school and having to ride the bus every day, and now, added to that, I was going to work too. It sounded like too much.

"I can't work," I protested weakly. "I gotta go to school."

"Don't I know that?" asked Mama. "This here job's for after school and weekends. My lady, where I work, has a friend with two of the cutest little kids you ever saw, and she's got steady help in the house, so you won't have to do no heavy work. You'll just take care of the kids and take them to the park and around."

I felt better. That didn't sound too bad, and besides, I liked kids. Maybe it would be all right.

"Do I get to keep some of the money to buy clothes with, like Alice?" I wanted to know

"You surely do," said Mama, "and you'll be able to pay your own carfare and buy your own lunches, and that'll be a big help. Besides, you'll be building references, and that's important."

"See!" said Alice triumphantly. "There you go, making sure that Ossie won't expect better than a reference from one white woman so's she can work for another white woman, cleaning slop and saying, 'Yes, M'am' and 'No M'am' all her life."

Mama fixed Alice with a beady eye. "When the day comes that all of you can be sure if you want to work at something highfalutin, you can get a highfalutin job, that's the day I'll say I'm wrong and you're right. Until that time, which ain't here yet, you all gonna know how to keep from starving, and that's that."

Alice subsided into an angry silence, and Mama, feeling she'd made her point, started in teaching me what I had to know about my new job.

"First off, tomorrow morning, I'm gonna take you over to Mrs. Fairbanks' house and introduce you. She's a very nice lady, and if you do your job right you won't have no trouble. There's just a couple of things to remember, and they're important. You gotta always be mannerly, with 'Yes 'ums' and 'No 'ums,' like Alice said, and you gotta keep in mind when you minding them children, can't nothing be more important. Children are a big responsibility, and you can't never go wandering off and leave them or forgetting to watch them careful. You keep yourself clean, like you been taught, and you keep them clean, and it'll be fine. Mrs. Fairbanks don't live far from the high school, neither, so it won't be no trouble at all for you to get there after school."

And that's the way it worked out. For the next year, five mornings a week, I got up at six o'clock; caught the bus at seven fifteen and rode the three miles to school; stayed there until two; walked eleven blocks to the Fairbanks' house; dressed Frannie age four, and Billy, age two; took them to the park if it was nice or played with them at home if it wasn't; turned them over to Mrs. Fairbanks at six; and then went home. On Saturdays I took care of the kids from nine in the morning till about three, when Mr. and Mrs. Fairbanks came home from playing golf, and then the rest of the day was mine. It was a pretty busy time, but I didn't mind it, 'cause Frannie and Billy were pretty good kids and they liked me as much as I liked them, and Mrs. Fairbanks was a nice lady who always treated me fair. Also, I liked having a little money in my pocket, and best of all, being so busy I didn't have much time to think about boys, which made me feel safer.

Then, toward the end of my first year in high, the Lord decided it was time for me to face my next temptation, and Aunt Mary's cousin, Livvie, and Livvie's son, Charles, came up from Georgia and moved in with us.

Charles was about the best-looking boy I'd ever seen. He was fifteen, like me, but he'd had his growth early and he was tall and looked more like a man than a boy, and his skin was creamy brown and his hair was curly, but not all kinked up. His mama was a widow and he was her only child, and she just thought the sun rose and set in him. She had more money than most because her husband had worked on the railroad and been killed in an accident, so she had pension money coming in steady, and Charles didn't even have to work to help her.

As soon as they came, Aunt Livvie took Charles down and registered him in the high school, but she really shouldn't have bothered. Charles wasn't any school-goer. Coming to our house was the first time he had even been near a big city, and as far as he was concerned, there weren't enough hours in the day for him to explore his new place, much less waste them in school, and, of course, he didn't want to explore alone. He didn't have too much trouble getting me to cut school with him, but when it came to my job, that was different. We set out every morning, like we were going to school like good kids, but somehow we never got there. It was fun, playing hooky with Charles, 'cause he always had money in his pocket, and with money in your pocket there are millions of things to do. We'd ride the bus into town, have a second breakfast in a diner down on Walnut Street, where we were allowed, and then walk to Fifth Street, where all the big shops were. Those shop windows! They were just as interesting to me as the movies we saw and just as unreal. There were dresses so pretty you just knew nobody could ever really own one, furniture set up in make-believe rooms that looked so perfect no dirty human would be allowed, shoes that couldn't help but make your feet pretty and hurting at the same time,

and millions of other things that were there for looking, not
for owning. I always kind of knew that the things in the shops
were never going to be mine, and so I could look without
suffering, but Charles wasn't like that. His mama had brought
him up to believe he could have anything he wanted, and he
really believed it, so when I stopped to look at something
pretty and just stand there, he'd get impatient.

"What you looking at it now for?" he'd demand. "You
ain't got the money to buy it, so what's the good of just
looking?"

"I like to look, that's all. Something that's pretty don't get
ugly just 'cause I can't have it."

"You crazy," he said flatly. "Ain't nothing worth nothing
if it ain't yours. Trouble with you, you ain't never had
nothing, so you don't know what it feels like." He looked
at me and grinned a funny grin. "Maybe some day I'll buy
you something."

I looked at him with surprise. I wasn't used to people buying
other people things. Why would he . . . and then, suddenly,
what Alice had said about lusting came to my mind. I looked
at him with new interest. He didn't look like he was lusting
after me and he didn't act like it, either, but why else would
he want to buy me something? I figured this was as good a
time as any to try out what Alice said I should do. I smiled
what I hoped was a sexy smile, looked at him from under my
eyelashes like I had seen Susan Hayward do in the movies, and
said, very low, "I sure would like it if it was *you* bought it for
me."

Something clicked in his eyes. I think, up to then, he had
just been talking to hear himself talk, but after I looked at him
that way I guess he saw new places to explore.

"Okay," he said, reaching for my hand. "Let's go to the
show, and maybe tomorrow we can figure out what to buy
you."

Boy, oh boy, I thought. Alice sure was right. He's lusting.

We walked to the theater hand in hand, and as soon as we
got settled in our seats in the warm, dark balcony, Charles
started his move. Up on the screen, John Wayne and a lot

of Marines were attacking an island in the Pacific, and Charles and I stared at the picture as though we were really interested, but what we were looking at and what we were thinking about were two different things. At first he draped his arm around my shoulder, like it just naturally fell there, and we sat like that for a few minutes. Then, like he was trying to get comfortable in his seat, he moved his body closer to the wooden arm separating my seat from his, and of course his arm and his hand moved with him. His fingers, which had been resting on my shoulder, were now on the side of my breast and, like he was idly keeping time to the background music, he tapped them gently.

Pretty soon, he stopped trying to pretend everything was happening by accident and he cupped my breast with his hand, gently squeezing and rubbing until I thought I would go out of my mind. It was right then and there I knew that I wasn't cut out to use lusting for profit. I didn't care if he ever bought me anything, just so long as he didn't stop doing what he was doing.

That day was the end of my just being friends with Charles. We kept cutting school together, but we didn't walk any more. We just made straight for the balcony of the nearest theater, no matter what was playing or how many times we had seen it before, and in the dusty dark we explored each other. I don't think we'd have come out until the theater closed if it hadn't been for my job. Charles was always furious and I even surprised myself, but somehow I just felt I had to be there every day, on time. In some way that I didn't understand it made up for what I was doing that was wrong, but, of course, Charles couldn't understand that. I couldn't even explain it; it was just so. Every day we'd come out of the dark theater into the bright daylight like two moles coming up from underground, and he'd go home like he was coming home from school, and I'd ride the bus to Mrs. Fairbanks'. When I got there, before I'd even touch the kids, I'd go in the shiny white bathroom and scrub myself like I'd been playing in the mud. Then we'd go to the park or play in their yard, and when the time came, I put them in their pajamas and gave them their dinner and then rode the bus back home, and by the time I got there I felt clean and like myself again.

We'd all sit down to supper together, Charles and Robbie and Aunt Mary and Janet and Aunt Livvie and me, and it was like the balcony in the movie theater was something I'd dreamed, but later when I was lying in bed next to Janet, all I could think of was Charles and what we were going to do together, come morning.

· 7 ·

IT TOOK FIVE MONTHS FOR THE TRUANT OFFICER TO CATCH UP
with us, and then all hell broke loose. Aunt Livvie, who
thought that Charles was the beginning and the end, would
have forgiven him anything, but not when it had to do with
going to school. She was convinced he had been born to lead
the colored out of slavery and although she wasn't sure how
he was going to do it, she had a firm notion that education
had to be mixed in there somewhere. Mama and Aunt Mary,
on the other hand, didn't set much store by my being educated, but they thought it was mighty important that if I was
pregnant I should have a husband, and by that time I was
pregnant. If we had stayed in the balcony it wouldn't have
happened, but when we got up one rainy morning it turned
out that everybody would be out of the house for the whole
day, so we left for school as usual and then, instead of going
to the show, we came home to that lovely empty house and
had sex. I didn't pay much attention to my monthly and when
I didn't get it for a couple of months, I just enjoyed being
without it, but by the end of the third month I noticed I
couldn't close the waist band on my skirt and I began to get

scared. That's just about how things were when the truant
officer showed up, and when Mama and the aunts found out
that both Charles and I had been playing hooky together
they started asking a lot of questions about where we'd been
and what we'd been doing. Charles was a good liar, but I made
up for him, and in no time at all I had blurted out the whole
story.

"They got to get married," said Mama firmly. "If they old
enough to fornicate and lie, then they old enough to get
married."

Aunt Livvie shook her head. "Can't get married without
Charles can make some money, and he don't know how to do
nothing."

"You don't have to know nothing to go in the army," said
Mama. "Lots of black boys who don't know how to do
nothing go in the army."

Aunt Livvie considered. "Might do you some good," she
said to Charles. "I never thought on how I'd let you come up
till now, but I can see I made some mistakes. Army might be
very good for you. Might teach you to keep your word and
do what you was supposed to do."

She sure didn't waste any time, once she made up her mind.
Next day she hauled Charles downtown to the recruiting
office, and before he knew what hit him he was wearing a
uniform. The ladies decided that Charles and I should get
married as soon as he finished his basic training, which took
six weeks, and that's the way it was. They sent him to Fort
Knox, Kentucky, for his basic, and at the beginning I think
Charles was kind of glad he was in the army. He thought he
looked pretty good in a uniform, which he did, and he enjoyed
being with a lot of men, 'cause he had spent his whole life
with women and it made a nice change. I was pretty excited
at the idea of getting married, and being pregnant didn't
really put a crimp in it as long as I was going to have a husband before the baby came.

About two weeks after Charles left for Fort Knox, Aunt
Livvie and Aunt Mary decided they had had enough of
living on the edge of a big city, and they wanted to go back

to Georgia. This hit Mama just right because she decided that with me getting married she didn't want to have to pay toward the house any more, so Aunt Mary could take Janet with her and Robbie, and I could get a flat of my own, from Charles' allotment. The folks Mama and John worked for were talking about moving to New York and taking them along, and this way Mama and John would be free to go if they wanted to. With Alice off at college and earning her own way, Janet with Aunt Mary, Verne still living with Grandpa, and me married, Mama felt she was free to stop worrying about us and go her own way, and she didn't waste any time doing it.

Everybody stayed around till Charles finished his basic and came home on leave and we got married, which was two days later. I would have liked a flat of my own, but John had a sister who lived in town, and she had a spare room, so Mama and John thought Charles and I should live there so's we could save for the baby. I was hoping that when Charles came home on leave he would object to that, but he seemed perfectly happy about the whole thing and we moved right in.

My wedding day wasn't much like it is in the movies, but I tried hard to feel like a bride. We got married by a Justice of the Peace at City Hall in Cincinnati, with Mama, John, the aunts, and Janet watching. Then Charles, who liked to throw money around when he had it, took us to a restaurant over on Walnut, and we had a big dinner with all the trimmings. Mama and the aunts didn't drink, but John and Charles and John's sister, Alvah, drank enough for all of us, and by the time dinner was over Charles and Alvah were slobbering all over each other and saying how happy they were that the three of us were going to live together. We almost had to carry them home to Alvah's flat, and as soon as we got there Charles passed out on the couch. There was a lot of good-bys said and then they all left, even Alvah, who said she was going to spend the night with a friend, and Charles and I were alone. I sat around for a while, waiting for him to wake up, but he didn't. I got tired just sitting there, so I turned on the radio and started dancing, all by myself.

About five minutes later, while I was prancing and twirling,

I heard a knock on the door. When I opened it I saw a girl about my age or maybe a little older standing there grinning at me.

"You're a pretty fair dancer," she said. "You been giving me a show for the last ten minutes."

"I didn't know anybody could see me," I said. "Where'd you see me from?"

She walked into the room, took in Charles sprawled on the couch and went over to the window.

"Look." She pointed across the court. "See that window right opposite? That's where I live. I can see everything that goes on in here. Just so's you won't think I don't do nothing but stand and peek, though, Alvah told me you and your new husband was coming today, and I was kind of watching for you so's I could welcome you to our swingin' building. My name's Cluny Collins, and you're Ossie White . . . right?"

Ossie White. It was the first time I had heard my new name said out loud, and it didn't sound like me, but from now on it was.

She pointed toward Charles. "This is the loving groom?"

We both looked down at him, sprawled every which way, breathing noisily and completely out of it, and the idea of him being a loving groom was suddenly very funny, so funny that we giggled and then, like sometimes happens when you're all keyed up, we started laughing, or at least Cluny was laughing. I found myself laughing and crying at the same time.

Cluny put her arm around me. "I know just how you feel," she said sympathetically. "Getting married's kind of scary at first. Took me three days to come down."

"Was your husband drunk, too . . . passed out like Charles?"

She laughed. "He wasn't passed out, exactly, but he sure wasn't feeling no pain. He didn't really sober up till three days later, when it was time for him to go back to camp. Most times, when you marry a soldier, you don't really have no wedding night until they come home the next time. There's just something about a black boy and a uniform that naturally leads to drinking. They all do it, leastwise all the ones I know, so don't be mad at him. He ain't no different than the rest. Meantime, while he's sleeping it off, why don't you come over to my place? Don't seem right, you just sitting here by yourself on your wedding day."

I looked at her doubtfully. "Supposing he wakes up? He won't know where I went."

"You can watch from my window. If he wakes up, he'll head for the bathroom right away, and he'll have to walk right by the window and you can see him. Okay? Besides, from the look of him he'll be sleeping for a long time."

I nodded. She headed out the door with me behind her. It seemed kind of funny, going and leaving him there, but Cluny was right. Just sitting alone was no way to spend my wedding day.

She led me down the stairs and out into the court, and I got a look at the buildings that were to be my home for the next couple of years. There were three of them kind of clumped together, built around a paved area, and from the looks of what was going on in that paved area, every apartment must have been home to at least five kids. Outside of a school yard, I never saw so many children in one place.

"Treenie! Gaylord! Come on over here!" Cluny was hollering. "I want you to meet somebody."

A little girl about five and a boy about three detached themselves from a bunch of kids playing jump-rope and ran toward us.

"These your brother and sister?" I asked.

Cluny laughed. "Brother and sister! Hell, no. These are my kids, these two and Danny, upstairs. He's three months."

I was so surprised I forgot to be polite. "You've got three kids? How old are you?"

Cluny reached down and picked up Gaylord. "I was seventeen when I had him, fifteen when I had Treenie, so there ain't no way to get out of being twenty now, is there? Twenty, going on fifty-five."

"Go on," I said. "You don't act like you feel fifty-five."

Cluny smiled. "I don't, but I always say that, 'cause when you got kids, you're never really young again. How many you planning to have?"

"Mama, I have to go to the toilet," Treenie said, ducking her head against Cluny's skirt. "I have to go bad."

"See what I mean?" Cluny started walking toward the apartment house. "Instead of dancing and flirting I spend my time washing clothes and cleaning bottoms. Seems like I never had no coming-up time. One minute I was a baby and the next I was somebody's mama."

I followed her and the kids up the stairs and into her apartment. It looked like she took in washing. There were diapers draped over all the chairs and even one hanging from the heat vent, and where there weren't diapers there were children's clothes. The whole place smelled like a laundry room.

"Stinks, don't it?" she asked cheerfully, wrinkling up her nose. "Today's wash day, and it's too damn much trouble to traipse down and hang the stuff out and then do it all over again bringing it in. I figure if I live here and I don't mind, anybody who comes in'll just have to put up with it."

I nodded like I agreed, but I didn't, really. I promised myself that I wasn't ever going to be that lazy. No matter where we ever lived, Mama and Aunt Mary kept things as neat as they could, and that's what I aimed to do now I was a married woman.

"Make yourself comfortable. Just push that stuff on the floor. It's clean. I'll go put on a pot of coffee. Nothing like the smell of coffee perking to cover the stink of wet wash. Treenie, you take Gaylord in the bathroom with you and see that he goes. I don't want no more wet pants to wash today."

I walked over to the window and peered across the court to where Alvah's apartment was. I was wishing with all my heart that Charles would wake up and give me a reason for going back. It wasn't that I didn't like Cluny; I did, but I was getting more and more depressed. If this was what being married led to—nothing but kids and laundry and no fun—it didn't sound like much. I felt just like Cluny said. I hadn't even finished coming up yet, and here I was a wife, and in four or five months I was going to be a mother and all my fun time would be gone, gone before it even got started. Suddenly all the thoughts about sin and temptation came back to me. If I hadn't been bad, if I hadn't lusted after Charles, I'd still be going to school, I'd still be Ossie Wilkins worrying about nothing and no one but myself. But I had lusted and I was getting punished for that lust. Then, like a voice spoke to me straight out of the Bible, I remembered what the Book said about it being better for a man to pour his seed into a whore than to pour it on the cobblestones, and right then and there I felt my spirits begin to lift. I was carrying a child, and that's what made my sin no sin at all. The Lord said "multiply," and that's what he wanted his children to do, and that's what I was doing.

"This here's Danny," said Cluny, coming up next to me with a fat baby boy wrapped in a faded blue blanket. "Ain't he fat, though?"

I reached out my arms and took him from her. He was so cute, with his shiny brown eyes and pretty brown skin, and he looked up at me with such innocence that I knew then and there that no baby ever could be a sin. I held him closer.

"Hey," said Cluny. "You holding him like you planning to keep him from now on. You got time to have a kid of your own, plenty of time. Don't rush it. If you ain't started yet, wait a while."

Until that minute, I would rather have died than admit I was pregnant, but now everything was different.

"Thanks for the advice," I said, "but it's a mite too late."

Cluny let out a delighted yelp. "Welcome to the club," she said with a big smile. "You gonna like it here, 'cause this place is just full of dumb black girls like you and me. You gonna be right at home with all the rest of us dopes who can't say no and probably wouldn't if they could."

Just then the coffee perked over, Danny woke up and began to cry for his feeding, and Treenie came bursting out of the bathroom dragging Gaylord by the hand and screaming that he wouldn't go in the pot but instead had gone all over the floor. I helped Cluny settle things down, and by the time things were quiet again we were talking like old friends, the old friends that we were really to become. I don't know what I would have done without her later on, when her strength and her sense of humor were all I had to rely on, but that day I just knew that I liked her. She told me that her husband was stationed at Fort Knox, like Charles, and he only came home on weekends, like Charles was going to be doing, and we made plans to keep each other company.

It was getting on to supper time, and I decided I had better try and wake Charles up. Cluny said she had had a lot of experience with drunks, and I should go home, make a pot of strong coffee, and when it was ready, pour ice water on Charles' head to make him wake up and then pour the coffee down him. I did just like she said, and it worked. I don't think he felt too good that night, but he managed to make love to me, and so my marriage started some like I had expected.

· 8 ·

THE NEXT FEW MONTHS WERE ABOUT AS GOOD A TIME AS I'VE
ever had in my life. Charles was at Fort Knox all week, but
on Friday nights he came home and was able to stay until
Sunday. I didn't really mind his being away, because I had
plenty to keep me busy. In the mornings after Alvah left for
work I cleaned the apartment, did the shopping, and had time
for a cup of coffee and a visit with Cluny. Then I changed my
clothes and rode the bus to Mrs. Fairbanks' and took care of
the kids, just like before I was married. Luckily, I was carrying very small and you really couldn't be sure I was pregnant,
because I just got rounder and rounder, like I was getting fat.

The weekends were really fun. Between what I was earning
and what Charles got, plus my allotment check from the army,
we had enough money to save for the baby and still go out
and have fun when we had the chance, and we had the chance
every Saturday night. There was a nightclub not far from
where we lived called the Stardust, and lots of black people
hung out there, and that's where we went. They had a five-
piece band and a dance floor, and you could always be sure of

meeting someone you knew, and it was a great place to go. I didn't drink at all back then, but Charles more than made up for me. As a matter of fact, this was really the only thing I worried about. Charles had always liked to drink, but from the time he went in the army he seemed to need to be drunk every chance he got. Alvah was quite a drinker, too, and from the minute Charles walked in the house on Friday evening until he left Sunday night, Alvah and Charles were some shade of drunk.

At first I pretended not to notice, 'cause Charles didn't take kindly to any criticism, and I don't like to fight. Besides, everything else was pretty good, and I wanted it to stay that way. I liked being married, and it looked like I had gotten over most of my guilt about sex and I looked forward to getting into bed with Charles and having him make love to me. I guess what finally made me start talking about his drinking was when he was too drunk to do anything but pass out when we went to bed.

The first big fight we had about it was late on a Saturday night about two months before Jackie, my first daughter, was born. A bunch of us had been to the Stardust—Cluny and her husband, Neel, Alvah and her current boyfriend, a couple of Charles' pals from camp, and the two girls they brought along. At home, Alvah and Charles had been drinking boiler-makers all day, and by the time we got dressed to go they were really high.

When we got settled at the club, I was busting to dance, because what Charles got out of drinking I got out of moving to music. I've been like that all my life. No matter how low I've been or how far gone in a pregnancy, when the music starts to play and I begin moving with the rhythm, everything else falls away and I'm free.

Anyhow, Charles was sitting next to me with his bottle tucked between his knees, out of sight of the table, pouring big drinks into his water glass. Some of the guys were old enough to order drinks, but the ones who weren't, like Charles, brought their own bottles and used them steady all evening.

I put my hand on his arm. "The music's starting," I said. "Come dance with me."

Charles seemed to be looking at me in the dusky light, but his eyes were so unfocused I'm not sure he saw me at all.

"Sure," he said thickly. "Le's dance."

Somehow he struggled to his feet, and I took his hand and led him to the dance floor. When he wasn't too drunk he was a great dancer, light on his feet and full of rhythm, but that night he could hardly put one foot in front of the other. He wasn't even really standing up, he was kind of draped on my shoulders, his head hanging over my back, and after trying to move a couple of steps I knew it was impossible. I kind of pushed him back to the table and we spent the rest of the evening with him drinking and me getting madder and madder, tapping my foot in time with the band and feeling sorry for myself.

It was about two in the morning when we finally got home. Getting out in the air had revived Charles somewhat, and he was able to get home under his own power. As soon as Alvah closed the front door, Charles made straight for the bedroom and I followed him in. He was tearing off his clothes and throwing them on the floor, and when he was naked he pulled back the covers on the bed and kind of fell in and closed his eyes.

By the time I picked up after him and got myself ready for bed I could see that he was dead for the night, and then I really got mad. I decided to wake him up, no matter how long it took or how mad he got, and I climbed in beside him and started pulling and pushing and tickling. He threw his arm out to brush me away, but he didn't open his eyes. That's when I started pinching his back as hard as I could and I guess the pain finally got through that wall of liquor that shut him off, because he pulled away from me so hard he fell out of bed, and that really woke him.

If I hadn't been so mad, I probably would have laughed, because he did look funny sitting on the floor as naked as a jay bird, rubbing his eyes and trying to figure out what had happened to him, but the way I was feeling he just looked disgusting.

"What you doing?" he demanded. "What the hell you doing?"

"I'm sick and tired of your drinking," I said with heat. "I'm tired of you being so drunk you don't even know I'm here, and I'm tired of sitting around waiting till you sleep it off, and I want you to stop!"

"Oh, you tired, are you?" he said sarcastically. "That's really a shame. That just breaks me up to hear that."

He pulled himself up off the floor and started putting on his pants.

"What are you doing?" I asked.

"What the hell do you think I'm doing? I'm getting dressed and then I'm going out, that's what I'm doing. You think I want to stay and listen to you tell me how tired you are? What the hell you got to be tired about! I'm the one should be yelling. If it hadn't been for you and my mama I wouldn't be in the fucking army, marching and saluting and cleaning floors. If it hadn't been for you I wouldn't have to be saving my money for no baby I don't want, neither! You listen here, you're damn lucky I didn't cut and run, and you better remember it the next time you get to feeling tired, 'cause it wouldn't take much to make me do it now!"

He grabbed his cap, and the next thing I heard was the slam of the front door. I just sat there on the edge of the bed, too startled to move. He had never said anything before about the way he felt about the army or the baby, and he always seemed to be happy with things, so I hadn't even thought about how he felt. It shook me some to find out I knew so little about him, and I began to feel like I hadn't been much of a wife. When I finally went off to sleep I had decided that tomorrow, when he came back, I'd start trying to understand him better.

He never showed up on Sunday, and even though it worried me some I figured he'd probably holed up with some of his friends and a bottle. I thought maybe he'd call before he went back to camp, and when he didn't, I called around a few places, but nobody knew where he was, or if they did they weren't about to tell me. By Monday morning I decided he'd gone back to camp, and although it was hard to wait a whole week to talk to him, I figured it was probably just as well that he had all that time to cool off.

Friday morning when I went shopping I bought all the things he liked best to eat. Then I went back home and gave the place a good cleaning, washed my hair, and set the table so's when I got home from work I could get right to cooking his dinner. I had talked Alvah into going to her friend's for the night so Charles and I could be alone, and I was more excited about that Friday night than I had been on my wedding day.

Everything worked out just like I planned it, except that it didn't end up mattering what I cooked or how I looked, because Charles never showed up. I sat alone in the apartment as long as I could stand to, and then I went out and started looking for him in all the places I thought he might be, but nobody had seen him and nobody knew where he was. I couldn't find any of his friends from the base to ask if he'd left to come home with them, and after a couple of hours of just going from place to place and finding nothing, I was so tired and so scared I just wanted to sit down somewhere and talk to somebody, so I trudged home and went and knocked on Cluny's door, but nobody answered. With a sinking heart, I remembered she'd told me they were taking the kids to visit with her mama for the weekend. I had no place else to go, so I went home.

By Monday I was pretty upset. Alvah kept trying to tell me not to take on and that everything would be all right and he'd turn up the next weekend, and Cluny said pretty much the same, but I didn't believe them. I figured he was gone for good, and after almost four weeks went by with no sign of him, I was sure I was right. I kept wanting to phone the base, but everybody said I couldn't, because it would make trouble for Charles, so I just waited. Then all on the same day, I heard about him from his mama and from the army, and both of them contacted me by mail.

The letter from the army said that Charles White, Private First Class, had been absent without leave for a period of twenty-eight days, and therefore I, as his wife, would not receive my allotment check. It also said that should he show up within the next three days they would review their decision. The other letter, from Aunt Livvie, was kind of hard to make out, but I finally deciphered that Aunt Livvie's sister, Martha, had gotten in touch with her to let her know that Charles, drunk and unmanageable, had showed up at her place in Loveland a couple of weeks ago and had gotten so sick he had had to be put to bed and nursed back to health. At the time of the writing, according to Martha, he was some better, but too weak to stand on his feet.

Loveland was only about thirty miles from Cincinnati, and as soon as I finished reading the letter I started for the bus station and an hour after that I was knocking on Martha's door. I had never met her and I didn't know what to expect, but the woman who stood looking at me in the doorway was the last kind I expected to see. She looked to be in her middle thirties, with a face like Lena Horne and dressed to kill. She looked at me coldly.

"I'm Ossie, Charles' wife," I stammered. "I just got a letter from Aunt Livvie, saying he was sick and here with you. I come to take him home."

She didn't say a word, just opened the door wider and beckoned me in. It was a big old house, kind of dark, but filled with pretty furniture. She pointed to a closed door, right off the hall.

"He's in there," she said.

I looked at her uncertainly, not sure she'd meant for me to go in.

"Well, go on!" she snapped impatiently. "Go see what you and his mama did to him!"

I walked past her and timidly opened the bedroom door. Charles, looking a little peaked but not as bad as I was afraid he would, was sitting in the middle of a big double bed smoking a cigarette and listening to the radio. When he saw me he smiled a big smile and held out his arms, just like nothing had happened.

"Hey, baby," he cried. "C'mon over here and kiss me. 'Bout time you showed up."

It was right then and there the mistake was made and the pattern was set, but I didn't see it then or for a long time after. I was so glad to see him, so relieved that he hadn't run off for good, so happy that I had a husband again, that I wanted nothing but to take him home and forget the whole thing, and that's what I did. Martha came in to help get him ready and she made some cracks about taking a child and trying to make a man of him before he was ready, but I was too happy to listen, and besides, Charles didn't take her seriously and kept joking about everything she said, so she finally stopped. Then, too, when we got home, Alvah and Cluny kept telling me what I wanted to believe, how he had to do it once to get it out of his system and how this is the way all men are, just like boys, and how now he'd settle down. We got in touch with the base and explained how he had gotten sick away from home and wasn't well enough to think to let them know, and, although they punished him when he went back by taking away his leave for a month, he got out of it pretty good, and they even sent me the allotment check.

Like I said, after he went back I didn't get to see him for a month, but then his punishment time was over and he started coming home for weekends again. By that time I was getting close to my time, and Charles couldn't have tried harder to make me happy and comfortable. He cut his drinking way down and he started talking about how he could work his way up in the service until he had a real good job so's he could take care of me and the baby in style, and I got to believing him, and I was happy.

Jackie came along on a Saturday night, which was convenient because Charles was home to take me to the hospital, and I had a real easy time, considering she was a first baby. The next morning, when Charles came to see me, they brought the baby in, and when he saw her cute little face he looked real proud, and I felt like we were a family.

The good time lasted just about a month. First off, Alvah said it wasn't the same living with a baby as she thought it was going to be, and she was moving out. I was happy she was going, because we really needed more room, but not having her there meant we had to pay all the rent by ourselves, so I decided I'd better go back to Mrs. Fairbanks'. I was pretty sure she'd have me because she had been very upset when I told her I wasn't coming back after the baby was born, but I was disappointed because I wanted to stay home and take care of my baby myself. I cheered myself up, though, with the thought that we could keep living in a decent place for Jackie to grow up in if I worked, and I knew she wouldn't be neglected because Cluny said she didn't see any difference between her taking care of her own three and adding one more of mine, so that part worked out all right.

The first couple of weeks after I was home from the hospital, Charles started drinking more than he had been, but not enough to really worry me, and besides, he kept joking about how he was only drinking to pass the time until he could make love to me again, and I liked that. The first night that I was able to, he held me in his arms and told me how much he loved me and how he loved to touch me and he set me on fire, like he always could, and when I went to sleep I felt so good and so safe. In the morning, it being Sunday, I took care of the baby and then made us a big breakfast and we sat around drinking coffee and smoking and just being happy. Charles had to get ready to leave for camp around seven, and after he was dressed he kissed the baby and then took me in his arms and held me like he was storing up a memory of what I felt like, and then he left.

Then, just like the last time, he didn't come back on Friday night. Unlike the last time, though, I knew right from the beginning what was happening, and I had a pretty good idea where to look for him. I figured he'd probably spend the weekend drinking and then when he had had enough he'd go to Loveland, to Martha, so I waited until Tuesday night before I called her. When she answered the phone she was even meaner than before.

"Yeah, he's here," she said, without even saying hello. "He come here last night, sick in his body and sick in his soul."

Anger gave me courage, "He's not sick, and you know it.

He's just sick drunk, that's what he is. And he's AWOL again."

"So what? What you and the army and his mama expect from this poor child? He ain't nothing but a baby!"

"He's no baby!" I said bitterly. "He's a husband and a father and a soldier and he's six months older than I am, so if I'm no baby, he's no baby, and you got no call to help him feel like one. If you wouldn't let him come to you when he runs away and you didn't make over him, he'd come home where he belongs!"

"That's what you think." Her voice was as hard as a rock. "If he didn't have me to come to he'd be out of the country by now, that's how bad he wants to get away from being a husband and a father and a soldier." By the time she finished she was mimicking me, but I was beyond caring. I only knew that he was the only security Jackie and I had, and he had to come back, and stay back. The urgency of my need made me tough.

"You just tell him to get himself together and get back here, or I'll tell the MP's where he is, and they'll come and take him in and they'll take you, too, for helping him desert."

I had no idea of doing anything like that and I didn't know if the MP's would even bother with her, but I must have sounded sure because she believed me.

"You ought to be ashamed!" she said half-heartedly. "You some wife, calling the police down on your husband."

I didn't even answer. I just hung up. I was shaking so bad I could hardly hold the phone anyhow, and I knew one more minute and I'd cry, and I didn't want to do that.

Charles came back the next morning, just as breezy and unconcerned as he had been after he ran away the first time. I tried to talk to him about how he felt, but he just wouldn't admit to it. Instead, he insisted that it was the liquor that made him act like that, and then he'd cut way down for a few weeks.

Money was getting pretty tight for us. Mrs. Fairbanks decided her kids were getting old enough not to need both me and the maid, so she gave me two weeks' pay and a very good reference, but I hadn't done anything about getting another

job because Jackie had been sick and she was slow getting
better, and I didn't want to leave her with Cluny all the time.
I really needed that allotment check, and with Charles being
so unreliable I began to have nightmares about not being able
to feed Jackie. And then, to add to my fears, I found out I
was pregnant again. I was afraid to tell Charles because I
figured when he heard that he'd run off for sure, but I just
had to tell somebody and, of course, the somebody was Cluny.
Meaning no harm, she told Neel, and the following weekend,
when Neel and Charles were both home, Neel ran into
Charles in the courtyard and started kidding with him about
how Charles was trying to catch up with him being a father.

Charles came back to the apartment where I had just
finished putting Jackie down for her nap. As I walked out of
the bedroom, he was coming in the front door.

"You want your lunch now?" I asked.

"I don't want no lunch. I gotta go out."

He started toward the closed bedroom door.

"What are you doing? You can't go in there now. Jackie
just went to sleep."

"Oh. Okay," he said. He seemed strangely listless and like
he wasn't really with it, not like he was drunk, but like he was
sick.

"You feeling all right?" I asked.

He nodded his head. "I'm all right," he said. "Don't worry
'bout me."

He walked to the closet and got his jacket and his cap, put
them on, and then walked over to me and kissed me on the
cheek.

"See you," he said, and he walked out the front 'door,
closing it softly so's not to wake the baby.

I felt pretty uneasy all day, but I tried to tell myself that
he wasn't going to run off again, that he had changed. I
waited until late Sunday before I called Martha, ready to go
through the whole lousy business again, but there was no
answer at her house, and when I called Monday it was the
same, and it stayed like that all through the week. By Friday,

Cluny insisted that I leave Jackie with her and ride the bus out to Martha's house, because she was sure Charles was there with her like he had always been before and Martha just wasn't answering the phone, but I knew in my bones it wasn't like that this time and I was right. The house was all closed up, and when I stood on the porch ringing the bell over and over, praying she'd answer but knowing she wouldn't, her neighbor stuck her head out of the window and told me there was no use standing there, 'cause Mrs. Williams and her man had gone away.

I don't know what I would have done without Cluny. All the other times I had felt he would come back, but this time was different, and if he really deserted, then my nightmare had come true and I didn't even have the money to buy food for Jackie, and what was I going to do about the baby on the way?

Cluny helped because she didn't try to lie to me about the fix I was in, but instead tried to figure out what to do next. She thought I should write to Aunt Livvie to see if she had heard from Charles, and I did, but before I could mail the letter, I heard from Charles direct.

He wrote that he and Martha had gone to his mother's but by the time I got his letter they wouldn't be there any more, and he gave me a post-office box number to write to if I wanted to reach him. He said that he just couldn't go on, either with the army or with the bringing up of a family, but that he still loved me and wanted me, and if I would do as he said, we could be together again. He had somehow gotten Aunt Livvie and Aunt Mary to agree that after the new baby was born I could bring both kids to them in Georgia and leave them there, and then go off alone with Charles.

"It'll be just like it used to," he wrote, "like it was when we first started being together. I want you to come and I hope you will, but if you don't you won't never see me again, because I can't live like we was living. If you really love me, like you said, you'll come."

I guess I didn't love him any more, or if I did it wasn't

enough to make me do what he wanted. The thought of leaving my children and spending my life running from the law was just more than I could bear, and I knew that no matter how rough it was going to be for me on my own with two children to provide for, it was better that way than the other.

It took me two days to write the letter to him because no matter how hard I tried not to, I'd start trying to make him come back, and I knew in my heart that even if he did he'd only leave again and there wasn't any use. Finally I got down on the paper that I couldn't do what he wanted, and I didn't add anything to it, and before I could change my mind I put it in an envelope and walked down and mailed it. Then I came back and sat down in my lonely apartment and tried to figure out how I was going to live.

· 9 ·

"I'M SORRY, MIZ WHITE, I TRULY AM," THE RENT MAN SAID, "BUT there just ain't nothing I can do. If it was up to me, why, I'd let you stay on as long as you have to, but it ain't. I gotta turn in my rents 'cause it's my job, and my boss, he don't take no excuses. Any time a tenant gets two months behind, I gotta ask for the key, so please don't make me any trouble. Just hand it over, okay?"

"What am I going to do?" I demanded foolishly. "Where am I going to go?"

The panic in my voice must have reached him, and he sat down on my couch.

"Don't you have no family you can move in with?" he asked.

I shook my head. "My mama's in Florida, and my aunt's in Georgia, and my friend Cluny's moved away, and I . . ."

I didn't mean to and I didn't want to, but I began to cry, hard painful sobs that I couldn't control. All during the three months since I answered Charles' letter I had managed to keep my feelings locked up, even when I had to accept eating money from Cluny, even when I came home after a day of fruitless job hunting, even when I crawled into bed alone and had to face a night of fear for the future. It wasn't that there weren't any jobs—there were, but they meant living away from Jackie, and this was something I had promised myself I wouldn't do. It was bad enough that she didn't have a daddy, she wasn't going to be without a mama, too. Then, like always happens when trouble sits down at your table, things got even worse for me. Cluny's husband was transferred to New York and of course she went with him, and then I was really alone. I tried writing to Mama, but every time I got the letter written I tore it up, 'cause I knew she'd tell me that I wasn't no different nor no better than she was, and if she could leave her kids to earn money for them, then so could I, and I didn't want to hear that, not from her or anybody else. I don't rightly know why I was so set on keeping Jackie with me but I didn't question it. It just had to be that way.

After Cluny moved I had to take Jackie with me when I went job hunting. All day, every day, I carried her from back door to back door while I hopefully answered ads for domestics, but when the lady of the house saw me with a baby in my arms and heard that I needed to live in with her, she shook her head and closed the door. I managed to eke out the little money that Cluny gave me to cover food and bus fare, but every morning when I went in the kitchen to get Jackie's breakfast I stared at the calendar on the wall, hating and fearing it because with every day that passed I was that much closer to being thrown out of the flat. It was only when I saw the calendar that I allowed myself to think of it. The rest of the time I assured myself that somehow it would work out, but it hadn't, and here it was, the dreaded day, the awful fact, the shameful word, eviction. It was more than I could face, it was too much, and I couldn't stop crying.

The rent man looked at me helplessly. "C'mon, now," he said, with what he hoped was a cheering smile. "Can't be all that bad. Always something a body can do."

I shook my head, the tears running down my face. "I've tried and tried," I sobbed. "Nobody wants help with a baby along."

Suddenly, the rent man jumped to his feet. "Your phone still connected?" he asked excitedly.

I nodded, not really daring to hope, but drying my eyes. He dialed a number and nodded with satisfaction when someone at the other end answered.

"Jessie? How's Aunt Phrenie today? The same, huh. Yeh, well, I guess no change is the best she can do. Listen, Jessie, you still planning on going back home if you can find somebody to take care of Auntie? You are, huh. Well, I think I found somebody for you. She's sitting right here, the nicest little lady you ever saw. You bet she's strong! Can't be more than about seventeen, eighteen years old, if that. Only thing is, Jessie, she's got a little baby and they both need a home."

He listened to the voice at the other end, and my heart sank. It was going to be the same thing all over again. Another turn-down.

"That's just what I was thinking, Jess," he said. "No young gal with a baby to take care for going to be flighty and gad about. No, sir! She'll be right there, morning, noon, and night. How about I bring her over there to meet you right now? Sooner you two get together, the sooner you can be on your way home to your young 'uns, right? Okay, we'll come now."

Beaming with satisfaction, he hung up.

"Like I said," he pointed out, "always something a body can do."

It sounded too good to be true. While I dressed Jackie I kept asking him nervously if his Aunt Phrenie wouldn't object to a baby, and he kept assuring me that everything would work out just fine.

"Aunt Phrenie can't afford to be so choosy," he sort of threw in. "She's a mite heavy, you know."

I had no idea what he was talking about and I don't think I was really even listening. All I could think of was that maybe, just maybe, I had found a home for Jackie and for me, a place where we could be together and not be afraid all the time. I wouldn't have cared if he had said I was going to take care of a wild animal or if he had told me it was the hardest work in the world as long as it meant that we could stay a family.

Aunt Phrenie's house turned out to be way over on the other side of Walnut Hills on a street of other houses just like it, well cared for and very old. I stood on the porch clutching Jackie to me while Burns, which was what the rent man said I should call him, rang the doorbell. It was opened by a young woman wearing a flowered house dress and carrying a broom.

"Well, Jessie," said Burns, smiling and pointing to me, "here she is, young, strong, and willing, just like I said. Ossie White, this is Aunt Phrenie's niece, Jessie Winters."

"Don't just stand there," she said. "C'mon in and close the screen. House'll be full of flies, you standing there with the door open."

We followed her into a big hall and then turned into the front room. There was so much overstuffed furniture, so many big wooden tables, such a clutter of glass lamps, bird cages, photographs, knickknacks and doilies that I felt breathless, closed in, and the fact that the shades were drawn didn't help any, either. Jackie, who usually was pretty quiet, picked that minute to start crying. Feverishly, I tried to quiet her, sure that any minute Jessie would say it just wouldn't do, but instead she reached out her arms and took Jackie from me, and Jackie, who didn't usually take to strangers, stopped crying right away and even smiled.

"I'll hold her," Jessie said to me. "You just go upstairs into the front bedroom and see if you'll be happy there. Then, if you like it, come down and go in that room across the hall there, and introduce yourself to Aunt Phrenie. I told her you was coming."

"I don't need to go upstairs," I assured her. "I'm sure the room will be fine. Couldn't I just meet Miss Phrenie now?"

Jessie shrugged. "Suit yourself," she said.

I started to walk out of the room, but her voice followed me. "Burns tell you she was a mite heavy?"

I nodded and kept walking. I had only one thought, to meet Miss Phrenie, be accepted, and know that I had found a home. I paused for a minute in front of the brown wood door and nervously ran my fingers over my hair and pulled my skirt straight, and then I opened it and stopped dead in my tracks.

Sitting in the biggest bed I'd ever seen was a brown woman so huge that she dwarfed everything in the room. There seemed to be no end to her. Her face was as wide as two faces: her arms, extending from what appeared to be a huge white tent, were like tree trunks; her body, outlined under the cover, was like a series of hills. I guess I just stood and stared. She was really something to see.

I don't know how long I might have stood there if she hadn't spoken, but the shock of her voice was even more startling than her appearance. Out of that mountain of flesh came a little, high childish sound that I had to strain to hear.

"You too far away. Come on over here where I can see you."

One of the tree trunks raised itself slightly off the bed and the pudgy hand at the end of it pointed at me, waving me closer. Hesitantly, I walked to the side of the bed. As I got closer I could see that what had appeared to be a huge face was really a small one set into a ring of fat, like a little picture in a big frame, and it was a face that showed that it had once been pretty. The eyes, hazel brown and bright, turned on my face.

"Bet you never saw nothing like me before, did you?"

Embarrassed, not knowing what to say, I just smiled. She smiled back and the sight was unnerving—it was like an earthquake was shaking up her face, with cracks scurrying in all directions.

"How come you want a job like this here one? From the looks of you there must be better things you could be doing than taking care of an old mountain like me so what you doing here?"

"Didn't Miss Jessie tell you about Jackie?" my heart sank. I'd thought it was too good to be true and I was right. She'd never stand for a baby in the house.

"Who's Jackie? Your husband or your boyfriend? That Jessie, she don't never tell me nothing 'bout anything. I reckon she thinks 'cause I can't get around I don't need to know nothing 'bout what's going on."

I shook my head. "Jackie ain't no boy. She's my baby girl,

and I need to keep her here with me, if you let me stay. She's no trouble and she hardly ever cries, and I'll keep her on the other side of the . . ."

"You got a baby? Here, in my house?" Miss Phrenie's whole huge body seemed to quiver with excitement. "Where is she? You go fetch her this minute so's I can hold her in my arms."

I guess I must have hesitated because I still couldn't believe she meant it, and, to my amazement, two large tears rolled over the enormous ledges of her eyelids and started the long journey down her cheeks.

"I wouldn't hurt her," she whimpered. "I'd be real careful and hold her like she was made out of china. Please, can't I?"

"Of course you can," I said. "I'll go get her. She's right outside in the front room."

Instantly her face went through that weird rearrangement that passed for a smile, and she watched me expectantly, meanwhile making little pushing movements with her hand, as though to hurry me up. I went out and closed the door behind me.

"Well?" asked Jessie as I came into the front room. "You staying?"

Happily, I nodded.

"She wants to hold Jackie," I said, stretching out my arms to take her.

Jessie looked at me doubtfully.

"What's wrong with that?" I asked. "Jackie don't weigh much and she don't squirm, either, and I won't let her tire Miss Phrenie out."

"Ain't Aunt Phrenie I'm worried about—she's got all the strength she'll ever need. It's Jackie. Aunt Phrenie ain't all there, you know."

"Now, Jessie," Burns interrupted, "you gonna have Ossie here thinking Aunt Phrenie's one of these here lunatics, and you know that ain't so." He turned to me. "She's just a mite slow, kind of like a great big kid on the outside and a baby on the inside, but she wouldn't never harm nobody. Never has in all the years of her life."

" 'Course she wouldn't harm nobody," Jessie said impatiently. "Not meaning to, she wouldn't. But sometimes she's like a baby, and she's so big you can't handle her, that's all I meant. Here, honey." She handed Jackie to me. "I guess it wouldn't do no harm to let her hold the baby, but you stay right there, hear?"

Holding Jackie in my arms, I went into the bedroom. Miss Phrenie held her just like she said she would, carefully and tenderly, and Jackie, feeling secure, took to her right away, and right then and there I decided Miss Phrenie wasn't nobody to be afraid of. She was just somebody to love. After a little, I told her it was time for Jackie's nap, and she handed her right over. I took the baby up to the bedroom Jessie said was mine and put her to sleep, and then I went back to the front room, where Jessie and Burns were still sitting.

"I'll tell you what your job will be," said Jessie, "and then you can go home and get your things while your baby's asleep. If I could, I'd like to leave tonight."

"That'll be fine with me," I said. "And it won't take me long. I ain't got much to git."

"You got to shop, cook, and clean. That's the easy part. The rest has to do with caring for Aunt Phrenie and that's real hard work, 'cause she's practically helpless and she weighs three hundred and twenty pounds. You got to get her in and out of bed twice a day and help her to the bathroom, and on the days she's feeling better you got to get her into the front room. How much you weigh?"

I didn't know for sure, but I said I guessed about a hundred and five.

Jessie shook her head. "Well, I hope you got strong insides, 'cause moving her is something else. She's partly paralyzed and she's like a dead weight. You think you can do it all right?"

She looked at me worriedly, and I nodded with a confidence I didn't feel. I was about four months into my pregnancy and I suppose if I'd had any place else to go I would have told her the truth right then and there, but I knew if I did she'd say I couldn't have the job and I just had to have it, so I didn't say anything, just nodded my head.

"My brother and I, we're the only kinfolks Aunt Phrenie's

got. Rawley lives here in Cincinnati and he comes over onct a week to bring the eating money, and he'll be the one to pay you. He works for the post office and he don't make a lot, so he can't pay a lot, neither. I figure seven dollars a week should be enough, seeing as you're getting room and board for you and the baby. If that's all right with you, I'll give you your first seven dollars now, 'cause Burns here says you're reliable and you ain't got no money at all."

I was so grateful that I almost cried. It all sounded too good to be true, and I wouldn't even let myself think that maybe I couldn't do it. I had to do it.

And I tried, I really did. Jessie moved that night, just like she said she was going to, and I was alone with Jackie and Miss Phrenie—and like Jessie said, that was the hard part. The first time I moved her from the bed to the bathroom I thought I was going to die right on the spot; but somehow, I guess because you do what you have to do, I managed to get her there and back. During the whole awful process she kept making little clucking noises and muttering about how nobody should have to do what I was doing and she tried as hard as she could not to rest her whole bulk on me. She was really a kind woman, and not slow, like Jessie said, but kind of held in by her body, like a person locked up in a jail cell made of fat. If I could have, I would have stayed with her forever, but I just couldn't. Every time I moved her I would get a pain like a knife cutting me in half, and I never stopped worrying about maybe I was hurting the baby inside me and I knew it was just a matter of time till I'd have to leave, so I never spent a cent of the seven dollars I got every week and I just prayed that I could stay on the job till I had a few dollars to see Jackie and me through until I could work again.

Rawley came around once a week, on Sundays, like Jessie said he would, and he brought me my money and visited with Miss Phrenie a while. He was a good man, steady and reliable, and it must have been hard for him, taking care of Miss Phrenie, 'cause he was trying to save as much as he could so's he could marry his girlfriend, who was a nurse over to the hospital. He was a kind man, too, and after a few weeks he began to notice I was looking poorly, and I guess it worried him, both for me and because if I got sick who would look after Miss Phrenie? I always told him I felt fine, but I guess he didn't believe me, 'cause one Sunday after I'd been on the job about ten weeks he brought the nurse with him. Like I said, I've never been able to lie good enough to fool anybody, and in no time at all she had me admitting that I was pregnant, and I thought she was going to throw a fit when she heard it.

She said I had to quit doing what I was doing right away, and then she went and told Rawley he'd have to get somebody else by that evening and if he couldn't, she'd stay till he did. She wouldn't listen when I said I had no place to go and nobody to help me; she just carried on about how the dumb colored all thought they were pack mules and that's why they were in the fix they were in. Finally, when I started to cry, she stopped talking and yelling and asked me if I had any money. When I admitted that I had a little, she said then there was no problem, 'cause I could live till I had to go to the hospital and then the county would see that the baby was delivered, and even though I was a mite run down now, I could hold down a normal job, but she didn't bother to tell me how I could get one and still keep Jackie with me. That was really my first experience with somebody who wasn't in my shoes, and never had been, telling me how to live my life; but it surely wasn't my last, and they all had one thing in common. They all wanted to help, but in helping they almost got me killed.

The next morning I packed my few belongings, dressed Jackie in her warmest clothes 'cause it was winter, and left. I wanted to say good-bye to Miss Phrenie, but the nurse said it would upset her, and even though I knew she was wrong, she wasn't somebody you argued with. Wouldn't do you no good.

I didn't want to spend a penny more than I had to, 'cause I didn't know when I'd be able to get a job again, so instead of taking the bus I walked. I had a suitcase in one hand and I was carrying Jackie on my other arm, and it was very cold out, so cold that the air hurt your nose when you took a deep breath,

and after a while it began to make me dizzy. The pain I had
been getting when I lifted Miss Phrenie came back too, and
just when I thought I couldn't go another step I came to an
old house with a "Room to Let" sign in front.

The landlady was an old brown woman with no teeth who
said she'd allow me to have a baby in the room as long as it
didn't cry too much, and the room was warm and middling
clean, so I said I'd take it. She told me it would be five dollars
a week, payable in advance, and I handed over the money and
sat down. I kind of held myself together until she went out
and closed the door after her, and then I practically collapsed.
Luckily Jackie was used to amusing herself, so she just sat on
the bed where I had put her and played with my purse until
I felt a little better.

I felt pretty bad. I had more or less convinced myself that
no matter how hard it was, I was going to stick it out at Miss
Phrenie's, 'cause it had been a real home for me and Jackie,
and I had hoped it would turn out to be a real home for my
baby, too. But now that hope was gone and I was right back
where I had been three months ago, except I had a few dollars.
Added to that, I had to face the fact that now I had to give up
the idea of keeping Jackie with me on whatever job I could
get, and that really wiped me out. When I tried to look at my
situation all I could see were closed doors, and I felt so bad
I crawled on the bed with Jackie, took her in my arms, and
held her until we both fell asleep.

· 10 ·

Wearily I pulled myself up the few steps to the porch
of the boarding house. It seemed like every day since Kim was
born I got tireder and tireder, and by the time I finished my
work at the cafeteria, tired wasn't a feeling any more, it was a
sickness, but it was a sickness I couldn't let get me down,
'cause that job—busing in that big bare eating place—was all
that stood between me and my two kids starving to death.

As weary as I felt, I still considered myself lucky that the
man who did the hiring had kept his word and given me my
job back when I came out of the hospital. It only paid seventeen dollars a week, but it had kept Jackie and me alive until the
baby was born, and now it was going to have to do for three
of us. Lucky for me, Erna, across the street, who took care of
the neighborhood kids while their mothers were at work, was
willing to keep Jackie for nothing while I was in the hospital.
Now that I was out and working again I had to go back to
paying her five dollars a week, but at least she said I could
throw in Kim for the same money. What with five dollars a
week for the room and five dollars for Erna, if I hadn't gotten
my meals at the cafeteria I couldn't have made it. As it was, I

wasn't quite sure how I was doing it anyway, but somehow day followed day, and night followed night, and me and my family was still there. At least Kim was four weeks old now, and leaving her every day wasn't quite as awful as it had been the first week, and Jackie was so used to my being gone during the day that she didn't give Erna any trouble.

There was an old beat-up rocker on the porch, and I sank into it. It was time to get the kids and fix their supper, but I just had to rest a minute, 'cause the five-block walk from the bus to the rooming house had gotten to me, and I felt like I was going to sink right through the ground. I leaned back and closed my eyes and kind of gently rocked back and forth, and I could feel sleep creeping up on me and I didn't have the strength to resist. All my pain started to drift away, and I was just starting to dream that I was a little girl again back with Aunt Mary, when a male voice cut across my relief.

"Don't you people do nothing but sleep?"

I opened my eyes. Leaning against the porch railing grinning down at me was a young man, a white man, with his white man's lousy way of looking at you as though you weren't real. All my tiredness disappeared, and instead of weariness I was filled with anger. What was he doing here in my neighborhood, standing there with his God-almighty face and his putting-down voice?

"Hey," he said, "you look even better with your eyes open. You live here?" He gestured toward the house.

I kept staring at him, saying nothing. I just wanted him to go away. He didn't even seem to notice, just kept right on as though we was old friends passing the time of day.

"Me and my mama just moved in next door, so we're gonna be neighbors, and maybe friends . . . that is, if you're of a mind to be any friendlier when you get to know me better."

Surprise made me forget that I wasn't going to talk to him.

"Why'd you want to live around here?" I blurted. "This ain't your kind of neighborhood. You ain't going to like it."

"My, my," he said. "I do hate to come across prejudice in one so young." Rage filled me, rage that I was too tired to control, and with rage came tears. I never did understand why

I only cry when I'm mad, but I was that way then, and I'm that way now.

"You get away!" I must have sounded like a hysterical little kid, 'cause that's what I felt like. "I spent ten hours today standing on my feet and toting trays out in your lousy white world, and I gotta do it 'cause I need the job, but this here's my neighborhood and you don't belong in it, so just get away and leave me alone!"

I don't know how he did it, but suddenly his whole face changed, went from looking white and disapproving to just plain sympathetic. He came around the porch railing, pulled a handkerchief out of his pocket and held it out to me like a present.

"Here," he said, "ain't no call to cry. I was just teasing you 'cause you looked so pretty sitting there. I didn't mean nothing by it. You just tired, worn out, that's all . . . 'cause if you wasn't, you'd have seen I wasn't really no ofay." He grinned suddenly. "They may be dumb, but they ain't dumb enough to live around here."

I guess I must have looked unconvinced. If he was funning with me before, how did I know he wasn't funning with me now? He saw the disbelief in my eyes, I guess, and he reached out his hand.

"My name's Augie. C'mon over and meet my mama. You see her, you'll know I ain't no ofay. She's darker than you are, but not so pretty." I shook my head.

"I can't. I gotta pick up my kids and give them their dinner."

"I'll walk with you," he said agreeably. "There's gonna be plenty of time for you to meet Mama. When she buys a house she settles in for a spell."

I was surprised; I wasn't used to hearing about people who bought houses. More usually, they were renting rooms, but I didn't say anything about it 'cause the way he said it, it wasn't any big deal to him.

I started down the porch steps, and Augie just naturally fell in next to me. Erna's house wasn't but half a block away, but he kept right on talking, and I found it kind of nice to be walking with a man again. When we picked up the kids he just naturally took Kim in his arms and carried her back to the rooming house for me, and since he was so nice I just naturally invited him in. He played with Jackie, who liked him right away, and he was easy with all three of us. When Kim had been fed and was in her bed, I gave Jackie her meal and got ready to fix something for myself. It was only polite to ask Augie to eat with me, but I was worried, 'cause all I had in the house was eggs and that didn't seem like much of a dinner. It was like he read my mind.

"I don't want to bother Mama with eating when she's just settling in, and I hate to eat alone. How about getting somebody to keep an eye on the kids and coming out with me for a sandwich? You'd be doing me a real favor."

I shook my head. I really wanted to go, but the exhaustion had come back, and all I could think about was how good it would feel to go to bed. He seemed to know just how I was feeling, and he didn't press it, and when I got to know him better I found this the greatest thing about him. You never had to explain things to Augie—it was like he could crawl inside your skin and just know what you was feeling, and there aren't many people can do that.

Of course, I didn't know that then, and when he started to leave and he said good-night to my little sisters, I made a big thing out of the kids being *mine* and my being glad they was mine. He didn't turn a hair, but I figured that would be the last I'd see of him. Of course I was wrong, which made me real happy at first and real miserable later on.

We got to be real good friends real fast. Even if you didn't want to like Augie you couldn't help it, 'cause he was the warmest, kindest, most natural person I'd ever met. He'd be waiting for me when I got home at night, ready to help with the kids, if that was what I wanted, or to arrange for somebody to keep an eye on them so's we could go out. If he ate with us, he always brought a big bag of groceries and he was forever seeing some toy or gimcrack that he thought Jackie would like and bringing it to her. Kim was too young for toys, but he paid her a lot of attention, and she loved him . . . and, in what seemed like no time at all, I loved him too.

Augie got to be so much a part of our lives that it seemed like he'd always been there, and like the dumb girl I was, I just relaxed and enjoyed it. He introduced me to his mother, who seemed a little too bossy, but nice enough, and he gave me back my being young just by the way he made me feel when he kissed me. At night after the kids were asleep we'd sit in the dark, happy to be together, and he'd rub my back where it ached from standing on my feet all day, and from that it seemed natural for him to make love to me, natural and joyful. I think he was the most joyful person I've ever known, and his love-making was just like he was. Augie made me feel like I never had to be scared again, 'cause there was nothing to be scared about. From time to time I used to tell him how it worried me that I didn't know where Charles was, 'cause how could I divorce him if he wasn't around, but he just said everything would work itself out if I didn't fret, and because I wanted to believe him, of course I did.

Even when I told him I was going to have a baby, he didn't blink an eye. He just took me in his arms and held me close and said everything would be fine, just fine. I kept waiting for him to say that he'd get a job and take care of all of us, but he didn't; he just went on taking money from his mother and bringing toys and groceries and such.

With a new baby inside of me, I was beginning to feel real worn out again, and it worried me that I wasn't going to be able to keep on working. One night when I was more tired than usual and pretty low, I decided that while it was very nice for Augie to be so relaxed about everything, he maybe was that way because he didn't know how bad I was feeling. He was lying on the couch reading the paper, and I went over and sat next to him. Unlike a lot of men, who don't know how to treat a woman, Augie always stopped doing whatever he was doing and paid attention to me right away, so he put down the paper and smiled at me, a warm, loving smile that made it hard for me not to forget my fears and smile back at

him. That's what was so dangerous about him—he was so
sweet and so selfish.

He patted the space next to him on the couch.

"What you sitting way over there for? C'mere, stretch out
and be comfortable."

I shook my head. "I don't want to be comfortable right
now. I got something I want to talk about, something serious."

He sat right up. "Okay," he said. "We'll be serious. What
you want to talk about?"

Because I really hated to upset him, I guess what I said came
out even colder than I expected it.

"I don't think I can keep on in my job."

There was a silence. I snuck a look at his face and saw he
was looking at me with a loving expression just waiting for
me to go on.

"Go on," he said. "What's the serious part?"

"Well, that's it" I was flustered. "That's the serious part.
If I don't work, who's going to take care of me and the kids?"

He smiled broadly like I'd said something really funny, and
put his arm around me, pulling me to him.

"You crazy, you know that? You the craziest gal I ever
knew. You eat with me, you sleep with me, you scratch my
back and muss my hair, and you don't know nothing about
me at all. Who you think is going to take care of you?"

I couldn't allow myself to be taken in.

"How you going to take care of us when you don't have no
job?"

"Don't you worry none about that." He started gently rubbing my neck. "I got my ways."

For once, the touch of his hand on my skin wasn't enough.
I shrugged his hand off me.

"What ways? How you gonna get money unless you work
for it?"

With a sudden move, Augie pulled himself to his feet and
for the first time since I had met him he looked angry.

"It's enough that I say I'll take care of you. How I do it
ain't none of your concern, and don't crowd me. You feeling
too poorly to work, you just quit, that's all. I don't want to

talk about it any more, either. I say I'll do it, I'll do it . . . my own way, understand?"

There wasn't nothing more I could say. I guess I must have looked upset, and he sat down next to me and pulled me to him, stroking my hair and soothing me like you'd soothe an ornery animal. I tried to stay apart from him, but the touch of his hand and the wanting to depend on him was too strong for me to fight. I pushed fear out of my mind and just thought about his words, and pretty soon my body began to think for me and then everything went away except the pleasure of our bodies pressed close to each other, and there wasn't any room for doubt or fear.

I kept thinking I couldn't work another day, but every morning something pulled me out of bed and down to the cafeteria, and every evening, dragging myself home again, I swore I wouldn't go back the next day. As far as I could see, Augie wasn't doing nothing different than he had been doing before—just being sweet and kind, buying groceries and doing things for the kids and not mentioning the conversation about his getting a job. Sometimes he didn't come around for two or three days, and I'd hope it was because he was looking for work or, better still, working, but then he'd show up as smooth as silk and not even mention where he'd been.

Of course, like I'd have known if I hadn't been so green, the time came when he just didn't show up at all. The first few days I missed him, but I didn't worry none. Then the few days became a week, and I started asking the neighbors if they had seen him, and none of them had. I could have gone to talk to his mama, but I was kind of scared of her, and besides, I wasn't sure she knew how close Augie and I were, but I found out when she came to see me. The one week had just about turned into two, and it was a Sunday afternoon. The kids were taking a nap and I was lying on the couch, so tired that my idea of heaven would have been to die right then and there if I could have found someone to watch out for the girls. When the doorbell rang, I thought about not answering it, but then I thought maybe it was Augie, and that thought gave me the strength to get myself off the couch and over to the door.

When I opened it and saw who it was, I just stood and stared at her. She stared right back, and finally I remembered my manners and asked her to come in.

She didn't say a word until she was settled on the couch, and the way she looked around her, like a storekeeper taking stock, I knew she hadn't missed a thing. I wanted to start straightening up, but I held myself back, feeling that doing that would only make it worse. The coffee pot was still on the stove, and when I offered her some she shook her head.

"This ain't a social call," she said flatly, "and it's not easy to do. I hear you been asking around about Augie, and I come to tell you he's gone and he won't be back."

I didn't say anything, just went on sitting there. I guess she was surprised that I didn't get excited or carry on or anything, and I think she thought better of me for it, because her voice wasn't so cold after that.

"Don't think too bad of him. He wanted to come and tell you good-by, and it's my doing that he didn't, but I know him better than you do and I knew it would just make it hurt more for both of you. He just can't tell the truth when he thinks the truth will hurt, and he ain't old enough yet to know that the sooner the truth is told the sooner the hurt begins to mend. What you aiming to do about the baby?"

Wearily, I shrugged my shoulders. I was too tired to talk, too beaten down to plan, too numb to care, at least for that day. I just wanted her to stop talking and go away so I could go to sleep and forget that I was alone again, and that Augie, my sweet Augie, was gone.

She got to her feet and started toward the door and, when she had it open, turned around to look at me.

"You think it's the end of the world, but it ain't. If you got the makings, trouble gives you strength, and if you ain't, it don't matter what happens to you. Augie's father was a white man, a white man that I loved and that loved me. It was different than you and Augie, 'cause I always knew he'd have to go away, but when he went he saw to it that I was taken care of. He gave me a house, and I've been buying and selling houses ever since and making money at it, too. I can't give you none, 'cause it's all in the bank for when Augie needs it, but I promised him I'd help you, and I will. The lady who just bought my house next door is going to take in boarders, and she's going to give you room and board for a year, and you don't have to pay."

She stopped talking and just stood there. I guess she was waiting for me to thank her, but the only thing I was feeling was loneliness and loss, a loss that was hurting enough to get through my tiredness.

"Why'd he have to go away?"

I wasn't even sure if I'd said it or only thought it, but she answered me, and she answered me with surprise.

"You didn't know? He's going to marry a white girl. That's what I been saving up for all these years, so's he can live where he belongs. He don't belong with me, and he don't belong with you. He belongs on the other side of town, and that's where he's going. I'm moving on, too, tomorrow, and you can move next door any time after Tuesday. The lady's name is Celia Johnson, and she's expecting you. Augie tells me you already got two little babies, so having one more won't be much harder. You'll make out. I can tell by looking at you."

She closed the door behind her and left me alone. I wanted to run after her and beg her to tell me where Augie was, but I knew it wouldn't do no good. I wasn't even eighteen, but I was beginning to learn. Begging and crying didn't change a thing. You just had to go on living the best way you could, doing what had to be done and hoping things would get better. I thought about packing, but I was too beat to do it right then, so I laid down on the couch and closed my eyes. I knew when I opened them again nothing would have changed, but maybe when I wasn't so tired it wouldn't be so hard. And it wasn't.

· 11 ·

CELIA JOHNSON TURNED OUT TO BE A NICE WOMAN, BUT SICKLY. She tried as hard as she could to keep the house clean and cook the meals, but you only had to look at her to know she was going to fall down in her tracks if she kept on doing what she was doing. Her husband worked as a porter on the rail-road and he was away a lot, and their five children were more bother than help. Finally, she had to take in a lady to help her, and the two of them decided they could make some extra money by watching some kids while their mothers were at work. Naturally, since I was already living in the house, they asked me if I would stop taking the kids to Erna's and leave them at home instead, and that's what I started doing.

I was still working at the cafeteria, because even though my room and board was free I had to have money and I had to save up for when the baby was coming. It had gotten a little easier, partly because I wasn't so tired any more, and partly because when the people at work saw I was carrying a baby they helped me out in lots of little ways. Things were a little better, 'cause even though I was lonely, I wasn't so scared all the time.

I worried a little bit about leaving the kids with Mrs. Johnson and Rena, the lady who was helping her, because in the evenings I'd hear them sitting together in the front room listening to the radio and drinking beer. Sometimes they drank too much beer and they got silly and loud, and once I had to put them both to bed. But during the day, as far as I knew, they never touched a drop. Still, it worried me, and I kept planning to leave work early some day and come home when I wasn't expected, to see for myself what they were doing, but my boss didn't like it when anyone took time off, and I was always afraid of losing my job. I kept wishing Jackie was old enough to tell me what went on when I wasn't there, but when I looked at her and saw that she was clean and fed and happy, I figured everything was all right.

I was just about into my seventh month when everything fell apart again. I got home from work one day to find an empty house—no Mrs. Johnson, no Rena, no kids—and Erna, from up the street, waiting on the porch for me. She hadn't taken kindly to my leaving the kids with Mrs. Johnson instead of her, and I suppose she was kind of enjoying what she had to tell me, but I didn't think about that then. I just wanted to know where Jackie and Kim had got to.

"Everybody's gone," she informed me. "Took 'em away, Mrs. Johnson and her lady-friend, and all her kids and your kids. There was a terrible row, and the police came, and then the county came and took 'em all away."

"Took them away where?"

I wanted to shake her. She looked so calm, and I was so frightened. "Down to the jail, I expected, and the kids to the shelter. Leastways, that's what I know they done before. Same thing happened to Ella King when she and her man had that big ruckus. Put the two of them in the jail and the kids in the shelter. You want your kids back, you gotta go down and get them. That's what the policemen said. I tried to tell them Jackie and Kim wasn't Mrs. Johnson's kids, but they just didn't pay me no mind."

Almost before the words were out of her mouth I was running for the bus. It was about three miles to the county buildings, and for the whole three miles I tried desperately to calm myself, but all I could think about was Jackie and Kim and how frightened they must be, and the picture in my mind of their two little faces like to drove me to a frenzy. When we got to the county buildings I jumped off almost before the bus came to a stop and ran into the first building I saw. There was a policeman standing in front of a big bulletin board, and I ran up to him. He was reading a big white paper, and he didn't even look up. I just stood there, and he just kept reading, and I finally blurted, "Please, where do I go to get my children back?"

He went right on reading, like I wasn't there. Deperately, I looked over his shoulder at the bulletin board and saw Juvenile—Rm. 246 with an arrow, and I followed it. There were big double doors, and I walked into what looked like a courtroom, empty except for a man way up front who was sitting at a table. He saw me standing, uncertain, in the doorway and got up and came over. I tried to explain what had happened, but it was hard to keep it straight because I just kept saying where are my children, I want my children!

"It's Mrs. Raleigh you want to see," he said. "Three doors down to the left." He glanced at his watch. "I hope she's still there."

Just as I got to the door of the office he'd directed me to, a lady was coming out. Breathlessly, before she had a chance to close the door, I started telling her what had happened. She put her hand on my arm.

"Calm down," she said kindly. "Nothing bad is going to happen to your children. Come in, and we'll see what we can do."

She led me into the room, waved me to a chair, and sat down behind the desk. Then she told me to begin over at the beginning, and when I was through she picked up the phone and asked for the shelter.

"This is Mrs. Raleigh, over at Juvenile," she said into the phone. "You have two little girls there, probably under the name of Johnson. One is almost two, the other eleven months. Their mother is here with me. I'll put her on. Will you please tell her how they are and please change their listing to the name of White."

She handed me the phone. After a moment a lady with a kind voice got on the line and assured me that both kids were having their dinner and didn't seem upset at all. It made me feel a little better, but not much. I just wanted to go to them and take them home with me, where they belonged. As soon as I hung up I turned to Mrs. Raleigh.

"Can I go get them now?" She shook her head. "I'm sorry, but it doesn't work that way. There are some things we have to straighten out first. Also, we'll have to see Mr. White. I'm sure all of this is just the way you say it is, but the law, which is there to protect your children, has certain requirements which must be met. To start with, you yourself are a minor, and, in a legal sense, your husband is your guardian."

Helplessly, I began to laugh. Somehow the thought of Charles, the baby who ran away, being my guardian was more than I could bear. Leastwise, I thought I was laughing, but maybe it was tears. Mrs Raleigh seemed to think so, because she came around the desk and patted me and handed me a tissue. After I got myself together, I told her about Charles and how I didn't even know where he was or *if* he was. "Well," she said, "that puts a different light on it. What about your mother? Where is she?"

I had to admit I didn't know. The last I had heard, she was in Florida, but I kept moving and I didn't tell her where I was, and we had lost touch. She looked serious. "Your being under twenty-one is the problem. In the eyes of the law, you aren't old enough to be responsible for the welfare of the children, and the court will feel they should be taken care of by the state until you reach majority."

"But I been taking care of them! All by myself, I been working and worrying and taking care of them, and we was making out. You look at them, you'll see—they're fed and clean and happy! Don't that make no difference to the court?"

"That's very important," she said kindly, "but the point is that the state has to look out for the welfare of its children, if it feels that the children will be safer in a foster home . . ."

"They ain't going to no foster home! They're my kids, and they belong with me, and that's where they going to be! Please, there must be something I can do! You know all the rules. Help me, please help me—we just got to stay together! That's what I've been trying to do the whole time, just keep us together. If Mrs. Johnson hadn't gotten drunk and the police hadn't come, the law wouldn't have taken my children away, and I'd have still been just as young. It don't make sense."

"I understand how you feel, but it *does* make sense. You left your children with someone who wasn't reliable, and in the eyes of the law that makes you guilty of child neglect."

"She always was reliable up till now! She never . . ."

"How do you know?" Mrs. Raleigh interrupted me. "Did you check on her? Did you ask the neighbors what went on when you weren't there?"

Miserably, I shook my head. The tears I had been holding back began to well up in my eyes, and the feeling of helplessness—that awful sense of being alone, just me against an army—started crowding me. Right from the time I had Jackie the most important thing in my life seemed to be for me to somehow keep us together, and when Kim came the feeling got even stronger, and it gave me the strength to do what I had to do. Without the kids, I was lost.

"There is one other possibility," Mrs. Raleigh said. "If you know someone, a respectable adult who would be willing to act as guardian for the children until you're of age, we might be able to get them released. Do you think there might be someone who would do that for you?"

Relief flooded me. There was a way! There was always a way, if you didn't give up.

"Sure I do! I know lots of people who'd do it."

"For instance?"

"I don't know who to mention first! Why, I can think of three or four right off the bat."

She looked at me with a little smile. She knew I didn't know who'd do it, but she was a kind woman. She stood up.

"All right, then, I'll see you here tomorrow morning with your friend. I'm sure we'll be able to arrange for the children to be released to you just as soon as we check out the reliability of the guardian you bring. We'll make arrangements then, too, for aid for you. With such young children you really should be able to stay home and take care of them yourself."

I wasn't paying any attention to what she was saying. My mind was racing, running, trying to remember everybody I knew, trying to sort out who might be able and willing to come back with me in the morning and say they'd be guardian for Jackie and Kim.

Of all people, it turned out to be Erna. When I got home she was waiting for me on the porch, sitting just where I'd left her.

"I see the kids ain't with you," she greeted me. "I didn't figure they would be."

Wearily, I sank into the rocker next to her. I knew I didn't have much time to sit, but just for the minute it was all I could do.

"You gotta find a gardeen?"

Surprised, I looked at her. "How do you know?"

"Ain't nothing to know. You ain't got no husband, you ain't got no mama, you ain't a adult, and your kids'r in the shelter—so you got to get a gardeen or they won't let you have 'em back. You ain't the only one it ever happened to, you know. Few other gals been in your shoes before you. Ain't no call for you to look so surprised. Trouble with you is, you never ask nobody nothing, just think you can know and do without no help from nobody. That's how come you don't know anything much about anybody else. If'n you had asked me, I could have told you that Mrs. Johnson and her lady friend wasn't no fit people to watch kids, yours or anybody else's, but you didn't ask, just went ahead and got yourself in trouble, and now you got to get out."

There wasn't much I could say to that. She was right. I had gotten so used to thinking of myself as being alone that I

made me even more alone than I had to be. As time went on,
knowing this about myself helped me spot it in other people,
particularly kids, but right then it just made me feel bad.

"You got somebody fixing to be gardeen?"

I shook my head.

"Well, if you want me to, I'll do it."

I was so shocked I couldn't think of nothing to say. Relief
flooded me, but then I remembered what Mrs. Raleigh had
said about how the guardian had to be checked out, and I
figured I'd better ask Erna if she knew about that. It was
kind of touchy, and I didn't want to make her mad.

"You willing to go downtown with me tomorrow morning?"

She nodded.

"They going to ask you a lot of questions, I expect."

She nodded again.

"This Mrs. Raleigh, she said they had to check out a
guardian."

"Don't have to check me out."

Stubbornly, I shook my head. She just didn't understand
what I was saying. "They do too. Otherwise how they know
you saying the truth?"

"Don't have to check me out," she repeated. "They already
done it, three or four times, I expect. Your kids ain't the first
ones I've stood gardeen for."

I was so surprised I stuttered. "You . . . you . . . been a
guardian before?"

She looked at me with disgust. "I just told you that, didn't
I? Wherefore you so shook up? What you think I was, some
kind of ignorant whore? I'm respectable and I'm reliable, and
I got money in the bank, which is more than I can say about
some people. I wouldn't be doing this for you, except I got
kinda fond of your kids, and you so young and hardheaded I
feel kinda of sorry for you, but that don't mean I can't
change my mind. You just remember that. What time we
going downtown?"

"Real early," I said firmly. "I got to get to work by noon,
otherwise I'll lose my job for sure."

"You even more feckless than I thought you were." Erna

looked amused. "You think you gonna get mixed up with them county people and everything go one, two, three? You ain't gonna get to work by noon, so forget it. You lucky if we all get back in time to go to bed."

I figured it was silly to argue with her. I just knew Mrs. Raleigh would take care of everything—she was that kind of woman. I was right about Mrs. Raleigh, but what Erna knew and I didn't was about how county aid worked. There were rules about everything you could think of and lots of things you couldn't, and there wasn't no way to speed it up.

Mrs. Raleigh handled the part that had to do with Erna and the kids, and that went off smooth as silk, 'cause, like Erna told me, they knew all about her there and they thought highly of her. It wasn't more than an hour after we got there that I was holding Jackie and Kim in my arms while Erna signed the papers that made her responsible for all three of us until I was twenty-one, and when that was done, Mrs. Raleigh said Erna could leave and take the children with her, but that I should stay and be signed up for Aid to Dependent Children. The kids didn't seem to be too shook up over what had happened, although I suspect they might have kicked up more of a fuss over my not going home with them except that they both knew Erna and liked her, but anyhow, that's how it had to be.

Erna said she would go by Mrs. Johnson's and get all our stuff together and move us over to her house, and she'd be expecting me when she saw me, and she promised to call my boss and tell him I was sick. We had to whisper about that part, because as far as Mrs Raleigh and the county was concerned, I wasn't to work any more, but while that sounded like a nice idea, Erna, who knew, said I shouldn't count on getting any money for quite a spell and I better try to hang on to my job until it got too close to my time. Seeing the way she knew her way around, and how Mrs. Raleigh and all the county people treated her, I decided she knew and I'd do well to listen to her.

I guess it was about eleven o'clock in the morning by the time Erna and the kids went home, and as soon as they did,

Mrs. Raleigh called somebody and then told me she had made an appointment for me to see another lady who was in the department that helped mothers with small children.

"I'll keep an eye on how you're getting on," she assured me when I got up to leave, "and when you're ready to have the baby, the county will arrange for you to go to the hospital. You'll see, it will all be fine."

She was a kind and well-meaning lady, and I think she really thought everything would be all right. I never did see her again, though, because I heard later she got transferred to another job where she didn't come into contact with people, just papers. It seemed a shame, 'cause she was an understanding woman, and they're not easy to find.

She directed me to a big room, a waiting room where I was to sit until my name was called. There were benches, but there were more people than there were places to sit, so some leaned against the walls or walked around, and others sat on the floor. There was a big clock on the wall, and every time the hands moved, it kind of clicked, and it clicked a lot of times before I heard my name. While I was waiting I kind of listened to the talk that was going on around me, and I was grateful that Erna had taken the children home, 'cause a lot of these women had their kids with them, and waiting for three or four hours is hard on a child and twice as hard on a mother. A lady heard her name called and got up from a bench right near where I was standing, so I got her seat and that helped some, and then as soon as I sat down, the lady on my left asked me if I had ever been here before. When I told her I hadn't, she said she hadn't either, and wouldn't be here now except she got sick and lost her job and couldn't pay for having her kids boarded out any more. The lady on the other side of me heard us talking and chimed in with how come *she* was here, and in no time I found out that I wasn't alone at all, that Cincinnati, and I guess every place else, was full of women trying to do the work of mother and father and sometimes needing a little help to keep from going under. Years later, when it became more fashionable to talk about how rotten black people had it, I sure couldn't argue, because it was true,

but I always remembered how many white faces there were,
too, in that county waiting room. At the other end of the big
room there were a lot of desks, and when you heard your
name you were supposed to follow the lady that called it
back to whichever desk she came from. Mine was called by a
kindly-looking woman with white hair who showed me where
I should sit and then took out a big bunch of papers.

"Now then," she said, very crisp, "the first thing is to get
your request form and your failure-to-provide form filled
out. You *can* read and write, can't you?"

Surprised, I just nodded my head. No one had ever asked
me *that* before.

"Here." She held out the papers to me. "Go over to that
long table and fill these out, and mind you, be sure to fill in
every question with a truthful answer. If we find that what
you say isn't so, you'll never be able to apply again, so keep
that in mind. If you have any questions about any of your
answers, you may come back and ask me, and when you're
done, take the papers and put them in that big basket at the
end of the table and then resume your seat and wait until your
name is called. Is that clear?"

The way she looked at me, even if it hadn't been clear, I
wouldn't have said so. I took the papers and walked over to
the table, relieved to have escaped from her.

The papers wasn't no bother to fill out. The only trouble
I had was on the failure-to-provide form, 'cause that wanted
to know about Charles, and there were lots of things about
him I didn't know, so I just wrote "don't know" and hoped
it would be all right. The white-haired lady had really put
the fear of God into me, and I wasn't about to say one thing
I didn't know for sure. I finished in a little while and put
the forms in the basket like she said and went back to my seat,
but there was somebody sitting in it so I went back to leaning
against the wall. The big clock kept clicking, and I was getting
hungry, 'cause I hadn't eaten but a roll and a cup of coffee,
but I couldn't do anything about it. All around me, people
who had evidently been there before and had come prepared
to wait were pulling out bags of sandwiches, and some even

had thermos bottles with soup. I could smell some of the food, and it made me even hungrier, so I started walking around to keep my mind off it.

Finally, about an hour later, I heard my name called again —this time by a man—and he motioned to me to follow him behind a big glass wall where there were more desks, but these were divided from each other by partitions. As soon as we sat down, he started reading over the forms I had filled out, saying "um" or "um, um" to himself until he finished them, and then he went back and started over. After about ten minutes of this, he laid the papers on the desk, pulled out some new ones, and looked at me.

"You understand that we have to check all of this out?"

I nodded.

"A worker will come to your house and see that you really *do* have the children you claim. Then, if everything you've said on here is true, you'll be eligible for about twenty dollars a month for each child, providing, of course, you stay home and take care of them. The money will go to Mrs. Erna Jones, who is listed here as guardian, until you come of age. Let's hope by then you'll have straightened yourself out. As an aid recipient, you will be entitled to have your baby at the county hospital, and your worker will arrange that for you. Is that clear?"

I nodded, but inside my head I wasn't saying yes. Even in the lousy job I had I was making twice that much and not exactly being rich, and I knew I just couldn't make it on that money.

"I can't tell you when the worker will visit you. We have many indigent and not enough social workers to go around, so it may be a while, but sooner or later she'll come. Now, do you have any questions?"

Yeah, I wanted to say—how do you expect me to be able to stay home with the kids if you provide money for them and not for me? I have to eat, too. I didn't say anything, of course. It was hopeless, and I knew it. It seems to me that somebody should have thought about that, but they didn't then and they still haven't. To this day, when a woman receives Aid to Dependent Children the amount she gets is figured by the child, and no notice is taken of her at all, and she's not allowed to work out of the home. It don't make sense, 'cause it makes liars and cheats out of some women who work and don't admit it, and wrecks out of the others who try to live on their aid and end up with barely enough to keep body and soul together. And either way, the kids lose out, 'cause they're either deprived of their mother or of a halfway decent life.

All the way home on the bus I kept my mind off how hungry I was by trying to figure out how the kids and I were going to live. Even if I could manage to work for another month, once I got near my time I'd have to quit, and then after the baby was born what would I do? Finally, when I turned it over in my mind a few times and didn't come up with any new answers, I decided that if we'd managed to survive up to now, somehow we'd go on whatever way we had to, and although it was small comfort, it was better than none at all. Just the thought that the kids and I would be together was enough. I had almost lost them, but Erna had gotten them back for me, so I had a lot to be grateful for, and I was young and strong. We'd make it, somehow we'd make it.

· 12 ·

ALMOST THREE WEEKS WENT BY BEFORE THE SOCIAL WORKER came. During that time I was able to go back to my job, 'cause I was living with Erna and she was watching the kids, for five dollars a week, like she used to. I paid her ten dollars a week room and board for the three of us, so I wasn't left with but two dollars from my pay, and I had to ride the bus to work and back. It would have worked out fine, once I got my aid, but of course that hadn't started yet. I knew I was taking a big chance not being there in case the worker came, but I didn't see no way out of it. We had to live, and Erna wasn't about to support the three of us, even supposing she could. As it turned out, for once I got lucky. They had started staying open on Sundays down to the cafeteria, so they gave the help different days off, and the week the worker came I was off on Thursday, and that's the day she picked to come. It was about ten o'clock in the morning when she rang the bell, and by ten in the morning Erna, who was an early riser, was just sitting down to her second cup of coffee. On my day off she gave the kids their breakfast so's I'd have one morning to sleep in, and they were all fed and dressed and

playing in the back yard, and I was in bed, sound asleep. Erna
opened the door to her and then came hot-footing it up the
stairs to wake me. She thought the worker would stay down
and look out the back at the kids playing, but instead the
woman followed her up and came right in my room. I had
been deep asleep, and being awakened like that was a shock,
and I must have looked simple-minded sitting there in bed with
the covers clutched to my chin and a strange lady looking at
me like I was some kind of lazy thing.

"Good morning, Ossie," she said. "I'm Mrs. Bailey and I'll
be your social worker. Aren't you well?"

The way she said it, I knew damn well she didn't think I
was sick. Some people have a way of saying something and
letting you know they're not meaning what the words are
saying, and Mrs. Bailey was one of them. What came through
to me was "what you doing in bed in the middle of the day?
Lazing like you're gonna keep on doing when you're living
on the county, right?"

Pride made me sound even shorter than I meant to. "Yes'm,
I'm well."

"What she means," Erna glared at me, "is she's well as she
can be, things being the way they are."

"Oh?" Mrs. Bailey turned a cold stare on Erna. "And what
do you mean by that?"

"She's fixing to have a baby pretty soon now, and she's
been feeling turrible low. Got back pains and leg pains and
Lord knows what all. It's a miracle she's able to get to her
feet at all."

"Oh." The explanation seemed to satisfy Mrs. Bailey. "Well,
in that case . . ."

"If you like to have a look at the chil'en, they's playing out
back."

I looked at Erna in surprise. Instead of the way she usually
sounded, she was more like the way the southern mammies
was in the movies we went to see. Absently, Mrs Bailey
nodded her head. She wasn't really listening to Erna, who
kept right on talking; instead, her eyes were taking in everything in the room, and she even opened the closet door and

looked in. I don't know what she was looking for—maybe a
man—but anyhow, when she didn't find nothing and satisfied
her mind there was nothing to find, she followed Erna downstairs. I got up and put my robe on and combed my hair and
went down, too.

"Ah jus' made a pot of fresh coffee," Erna was saying in
that slow, silly way. "Ah'd be honored if'n you'd have a cup."

"No, thank you." Mrs. Bailey's tone said she'd rather be
caught dead than drinking coffee with the likes of us. "When
is your baby due?"

"In about three, four weeks, I reckon."

She raised her eyebrows. "You reckon? Don't you *know?*
What did the doctor tell you?"

"I ain't had no call to see a doctor."

"But this woman says you're too sick to stand up! And
besides, you should be seeing the doctor down at County,
anyhow. You people just don't take care of yourselves, and
then when you're too sick to work you expect to be taken
care of by people who work hard and pay taxes. No one minds
giving to people who really have tried their best and through
unfortunate circumstances need help, but to just not even
try . . ."

I opened my mouth, but before I could say anything, Erna
jumped in.

"It ain't that Ossie didn't wanta see a doctor! No, m'am,
that wasn't the case at all. It was the other way to. She thought
that until you been here and okay'd her for aid she couldn't
see the doctor at county. Ain't that right, Ossie?" I barely
nodded. I could see what Mrs. Bailey thought of me by the
expression in her eyes, and I hoped she could read mine as easy.

"I'll turn in my report," said Mrs. Bailey, "but it may be two
or three weeks more before it all goes through. In the meantime, though, you may go to the obstetrical clinic at county.
Just tell them that I'm assigned to your case, and I told you
to come. Is that clear?"

I guess when these social workers got trained they must
have been told to always end up with "is that clear?" Maybe
they didn't mean anything by it, but it sure made you feel

like a dope, like you were too stupid to understand English. I just nodded again. I've heard tell that a lot of whites say blacks are sullen, but I wonder if those whites ever listen to themselves and hear how they sound. When somebody's picking at your soul with his voice, you just naturally cover it up and try to keep it whole.

Mrs. Bailey poked around some more, went out in the back and watched the kids for a few minutes, and then acted like she'd done her duty and was fixing to leave.

"Now don't you forget to go to the O.B. clinic," she said to me as she was leaving. "The least you can do is take proper care of yourself now, so you'll be able to care for all your children later. Irresponsibility is what got you in this fix in the first place, you know."

My face must have shown the disgust I felt for her, 'cause Erna rushed in again like she was the cavalry heading 'em off at the pass.

"Doan you worry none. She gonna take care of herself, 'cause ol' Erna's here to see that she do, an' besides, she's a gal what wanta do right, ain't you, Ossie?"

Before I could get my mouth open, Erna gently eased Mrs. Bailey out the door and shut it firmly behind her. Then she turned to me, her eyes blazing.

"What's the matter with you? Ain't you got the sense you was born with? Don't you know how to handle them people yet? No, not you—you get up on your high horse, stick your nose in the air, and starve." She shook her head in real disgust. "I didn't know you was so dumb."

"I'm not dumb!" I said, angrily. "I'm just not an ass-kissin' black worm like you want me to be. The kids and I ain't starved up to now, and we ain't gonna, and if I have to act like you just did to get that crummy little bit of money they call aid, then I'll just get along without it."

"You fool," Erna said flatly. "You care what they think of you? Then you a fool. They don't even see you. You ain't Ossie White, a real person, you just a nigger, another shiftless nigger who got to be handed out to, and if they didn't need to think about themselves as Christians, they'd just as soon kill you as look at you. We're in bondage, just as much as we was before the War between the States, only now the massa don't live in the big white house on the hill, he lives in the county office, and instead of handing out rations and aprons and clean head rags, he hands out aid checks. That's the only difference."

Suddenly I was a little girl, back standing in the Georgia sunshine listening to my grandfather.

"About all a man's got in this world is his self-respect," he had said, "and can't nobody take that away from him but him."

"What about how you feel about yourself?"

Erna shook her head disgustedly. "That's what I'm talking about, if you'd just listen. Those aid people, they don't really look at you, they just look at a picture in their mind, and that picture gonna stay, no matter what you do, so you help the picture along, and all the time, inside of you, you laughing 'cause they so blind. You gotta do with what you got, and if you living in a white man's world, why then you do everything you hafta to get the most you can, that's all. And you keep on laughing."

I kind of felt there was something wrong with what she was saying, but at that minute I couldn't put my finger on it, so I just let it go at that. I knew one thing for sure, though. Whether she was right or not, it didn't really make no nevermind to the way I acted, 'cause something inside made it out of the question for me to act that way too.

Later that same day I did as I was told and went to the clinic at the county hospital, where they told me what I already knew, that I was going to have a baby in about three or four weeks. After the doctor examined me and I had put my clothes back on he said, "You're not even nineteen yet and you're about to have your third child. At this rate, by the time you go through the menopause, which will be about twenty-five years from now, you'll be the mother of at least twenty, or maybe more. Is that what you want?"

I thought he was joking, so I just laughed and shook my head but he was dead serious.

"Well, all right then. What are you going to do about preventing it?"

I didn't want to talk about it. The whole subject wasn't none of his business, as far as I could see, so I figured the best way was to go on joking, and maybe he'd leave me alone.

"Sleep alone?"

He looked impatient. "That's no answer, and you know it. You're not stupid and you're young enough to learn, so you haven't any excuse to go on filling the world with children you can't take care of properly. Even if you could take care of them, there are just too many people on earth anyhow. You know, when you come in to have your baby, we could tie your tubes. It's a very simple thing to do, won't cause you any problems later, and you just won't get pregnant any more."

"I don't know," I lied. I *did* know. Nobody was going to do anything like that to me. It said in the Bible that even a fallen woman wasn't no whore if she populated the earth, and besides, what he said about my not being able to take care of the kids, no matter how many I had, just wasn't true. I'd managed up to now, and I'd go on managing. He scared me, though.

"Well, you think about it. We can't do it without your husband's permission, you know, so maybe you better talk it over with him."

Relief was like a nice warm blanket. If they needed permission from Charles, then I was safe, 'cause nobody knew where he was. Maybe there was something in what Erna said, 'cause when I left the clinic I was promising the doctor I'd think about having my tubes tied, but inside I was laughing.

I worked right up till the week before Anthony was born, and it didn't hurt me none. He was a healthy boy, weighing almost eight pounds, and I didn't have no trouble, and I felt pretty good in the hospital 'cause it looked like my worst troubles was over. Now that Erna was around, I didn't feel so alone any more, and I didn't have to worry about the kids bein' all right when I went back to work, 'cause she took real good care of them. By the time Anthony was two weeks old, my first aid check came, and with that and what I could make at the cafeteria, everything looked like it was going to be easier. I started being able to buy clothes for the kids, and I even got a new dress for myself, the first one I'd had since the beginning of my marriage to Charles. I guess I was looking pretty good, 'cause pretty soon, when I sat on the front porch in the evening, some of the boys and men in the neighborhood started drifting over, and it felt so good to joke and laugh and be young again.

Mostly they was about my age, but there were a couple of men in their thirties who would come by from time to time, and I liked them the best of all. One of them, Jim, reminded me of my stepfather, and I felt real easy and safe with him. Some of the others, hoping to make him look bad to me, I guess, told me he had a wife, but I wasn't fixing to get married, so I didn't care. We was just funning, anyhow, so what was the harm? I figured when the weather got cold and I couldn't sit out any more, the whole thing would kind of peter out, and it mostly did. The boys went back to going to the pool room, and I don't know what happened to Brown, the other man, but Jim kept coming over and keeping me company. He never mentioned his wife, or how come he wasn't home with her, and it didn't seem polite to me to bring it up, 'cause I figured if he wanted to talk about her he would.

At first he just came for an hour or so and passed the time of day, and then, little by little, he stayed longer and longer. I loved having him around 'cause he had traveled all over the country when he worked for the railroad, and he told me about how it was in other places, and he could really tell it. He seemed to remember everything he ever saw, and he had the gift of tongues; when he described a place you felt like you'd been there. He was a real gentleman and he never even tried to kiss me. Even Erna, who didn't approve of the whole thing, couldn't find anything to make a fuss about, and Erna could make a fuss about almost anything.

After about three months of him coming and sitting and talking about where he'd been, he asked me if I'd like to see a movie about some of the places he had mentioned. Down to the school there was going to be some travel pictures, and he was going. I said I sure would and he said he'd come by for me on Friday about seven thirty and we'd go. Erna, who was passing through the front room, heard him ask me.

"That'll be right nice for Ossie," she said. "She don't hardly get out of this house at all, less'n she's working."

I looked at her suspiciously. I didn't know what she was up to, but I knew I wasn't going to like it. Jim, who didn't know her like I did, looked glad that she liked the idea.

"Maybe when the movie's over you and your woman can come back with Ossie and have coffee with me. It'd pleasure me to meet her and tell her how nice you been."

Jim looked so uncomfortable that I wanted to cry, and Erna looked like the cat who'd licked up the cream. She knew I was mad, so she didn't look my way at all, just kept looking at Jim with big, innocent eyes and a nice smile. All of a sudden, I think Jim caught on to what she was doing.

"My wife won't be with me," he said quietly. "She don't go out hardly at all since the accident."

He didn't say anything more, and I hoped that Erna would go on and ask him some questions, 'cause I really wanted to know, but, contrary thing that she was, she just said something about that being a shame, and walked out of the room. I was busting with curiosity, and I suppose Jim knew I was, 'cause he said, real low, "Her face got all cut up in a car accident and it's like she's dead. Won't go nowhere, won't let anybody come to see her, don't even want to see me. She keeps the blinds closed and sits in the house all alone, except for the dog. It's driving me crazy, too. I want to just go away. Keep sending her money, but go away, and I know that ain't right. That's why I started calling on you. It ain't harming nobody, and it keeps me from feeling like I'm dead, too. I never lied about being married, and you didn't seem to mind, so I just kept on coming. If you've changed your mind about it, well, you just have to tell me, that's all."

I shook my head. "I don't see why I should do that. I got a husband but nobody knows where he is, so he's not doing me much good, and you got a wife but she's a invalid, so she ain't doing you much good, and you say she don't even want you around much, so you ain't taking away from her to see me. When you get here Friday night, I'll be ready and waiting."

Nothing more was said about it, and we just went back to talking about what we usually did, but I felt like we had made some kind of promise to each other, and it was the kind of promise I've always liked, where two people having it tough kind of join up to make it a little easier.

· 13 ·

Different times in your life have their own special feelings when you think back on them, and no matter how worried and upset I've been since, when I think back on when I was living with Erna and loving with Jim, I feel calmer and safer and more alive. I guess it was the only time in my life when I knew what it felt like to just go from day to day, not having to worry too much about keeping me and the kids alive, being loved by a man who could set me on fire just by touching me, not caring and not needing to care about much but what was nice things.

It was like being married, only nicer. Jim was my lover and my friend, and he was crazy about the kids, specially Anthony, so of course the kids was crazy about him. When you're nineteen and lustful, like I was, and you haven't been with a man for a spell, maybe you don't think about it when it ain't happening, but then, when it does happen again, you like to explode. Jim knew how to pleasure a woman, and I was a woman that could be pleasured, so when we come together, it was like a firecracker going off. Erna grumbled some when she first saw how it was with us, but after a while we was so happy that it showed, and she just left off making faces and mean remarks and let us be. Jim was always telling Erna how meeting me saved his life, 'cause between his wife being so depressed and his having to work in a restaurant downtown instead of on the dining cars, like he always did before she was hurt and he had to stay home with her, he had been thinking of cutting and running, but meeting me had made the difference. I didn't really believe him when he said that, 'cause he wasn't a man to run away, but it did make me feel good and important, and when you feel like that, you don't fight it.

We had about three or four months like that and I was just beginning to believe I wouldn't ever be alone any more when Erna took sick. I had been noticing that she wasn't as chipper as always, but she didn't complain none, and I was too happy to worry for long, so I wasn't as caring as I should have been. One morning when I was leaving for work she came down the stairs real slow, and when she got to the bottom she made a low moaning sound, grabbed for the railing, missed, and fell on her face. I dragged her to a chair and tried fanning her and getting her to take some water, but she just kept moaning and clutching her chest, and her skin was such a funny ashy-gray color that I knew I better get some help. I ran up to the corner to the telephone and called the county, and they said they'd send an ambulance, and then I ran back as fast as I could. Jackie was standing looking at Erna, and the way Erna looked got her so upset she started to cry, and when Jackie cried Kim cried too, just on general principles, so they was both standing there just sobbing. I quieted them down and sent them out to play, and by that time the ambulance come. The doctor listened to Erna's chest and said something about a coronary something, and they put her on a stretcher and started to carry her out. I tried to talk to her, but her eyes were closed, and the doctor waved me away and they was gone. I called the cafeteria and told them I couldn't come in, and why, and they said all right, but I better be there tomorrow.

I spent the whole day trying to find somebody to leave the

kids with and, in between, calling the county to find out how Erna was doing, but I didn't have much success with either thing. There was a lady down the street who said she'd watch the kids for me, and I knew I'd have to let her if I couldn't find nobody else, but she had ten children of her own, and I wasn't easy in my mind about it. The hospital kept saying Erna was doing as well as could be expected, which didn't really tell me anything, but that's all they said, so there wasn't anything I could do about that, and I had to lie and say I was her niece before they'd even tell me that. After supper, when Jim came over, he sat with the kids and I went down to the hospital, but it was a long trip for nothing, 'cause Erna couldn't have any visitors. I got pretty frightened when I asked about her, because the nurse called the doctor, and he said she was critical, and did I know of any relatives who should be called. I said as far as I knew, Erna had a sister in North Carolina and that was all, and they didn't even write to each other. He wanted to know if I could be reached by phone, so I gave him Jim's number, and then he said I should go home. I didn't want to; I wanted to be there in case Erna woke up, but the doctor said she wouldn't 'cause they were keeping her asleep.

Early in the morning Jim came knocking at my door. He said he'd called county and said he was a relative, and they told him that Erna was still alive and that was a good sign, but she still couldn't have visitors. I told him about taking the kids to Mrs. Walters, the lady with the ten children, and he agreed there wasn't nothing else I could do, so while Jackie and Kim was eating their breakfast and I was giving Anthony his bottle I tried to explain to them about Erna being sick in the hospital and not able to look after them, and their having to go to Mrs. Walters' house until I came home from work. Jackie didn't cry, just looked like she might, so Kim didn't either, and that helped.

Thank God, Erna didn't die, but she was awful sick for a long time, and she never really got better, like the way she was before. The people at the county located her relatives in North Carolina, and I guess they decided that the best thing to do

would be to sell her house and take her home with them.
Erna didn't want to do that at first, mainly on account of me
and the kids, but she was really too sick to put up much of a
struggle, and in the long run it was the best thing to do. When
I went to the hospital to see her I acted like it didn't make
no difference to me about where I lived as long as she got to
feeling better, but of course it made all the difference in the
world. Living with Erna I had been starting to feel like I was
back with my family again, with people around who gave
a damn about me and what happened to me, and it helped a
lot, but, like most things you like, it didn't last long. Anyhow,
they did sell the house and I had to go back to living in a room
with the kids, and that meant that Jim and I had no place to
go to be alone.

Erna wouldn't go away without saying good-by to me and
the kids, so on my day off, which was the day before she was
being discharged from the hospital, we all went down to see
her. They didn't let kids upstairs, so they wheeled her down
to the lobby and said she could have about fifteen minutes
with us, and it was too short a time and too long a time. Erna
had been so good to us and she really loved the kids, and it
was rough to know that we probably wouldn't see each other
again. All that was bad enough, and then, to top it off, she
reminded me not to let the welfare know that she had moved
away, 'cause if they found out the children's guardian wasn't
around any more they'd put the kids in foster homes for sure.
I had been so worried about her I just hadn't thought of that
part before, and it terrified me, but then I remembered Jim,
and I knew he'd help me, so I told Erna not to worry, that
everything would be all right. When I said that, she looked
at me like the old Erna, full of vinegar and believing nothing.

"You ain't gonna take my advice, are you?" she said. It
wasn't no question, it was a statement.

"Well, I would, excepting I don't have to on account of
Jim, you know. It's better not to lie to the county if you
don't have to, ain't it?"

She nodded. "If you don't have to, sure it's better. But it's better still not to take chances with money you need, and most of all, with whether they let you keep your kids."

I looked at her with surprise. "How come you think they'd take the kids away? Jim's a respectable, reliable adult, same as you, so why shouldn't he be guardian for us for a while?"

Suddenly Erna looked very tired. "If you don't know about men by now, my telling you ain't going to make no difference. You just do the best you can, and maybe things'll work out, and maybe they won't. Don't finally make much difference, anyhow."

"Don't you worry," I said soothingly. "We'll all make out fine. You'll go home and have a long rest, and when you come back we'll all live together again just like it was before."

She kissed the kids and me, and we cried a little, and then the nurse came to wheel her back upstairs. She turned around in her chair and waved to us just before the elevator door closed behind her, and that's the last time I ever saw her. She didn't leave nobody behind who kept tabs on her, so I never heard what happened to her but she was like a mother to me, and I'll never forget her. And just like as if she was my real mother, I didn't listen to her when she gave me advice, and she was right and I was wrong.

It wouldn't have been so bad if Jim had told me the truth straight out, but he didn't. When I first told him about Erna being the guardian for us and how, now that she was going away, we'd need a new one, he just smiled and didn't say yes and didn't say no, but I needed to believe he'd do it, so I just concentrated on the yes. I suppose if someone was to ask me what was the dumbest thing I did more than once in my life, I'd have to say that it was only hearing what I wanted to hear. That can get you in more trouble than stepping in a hornets' nest without your shoes.

Jim didn't come around as often as he had before, but I didn't think nothing of it, because with me living in one room with the kids we didn't have space to spread out and be comfortable like we was before, and Jim said the kids being in the room with us made him nervous, although it didn't bother me none. Whenever he did come, I'd ask him when he could go down to the welfare with me to sign the papers for being a guardian, and he'd say next week for sure, but when next week came he couldn't make it.

When the first check came, right after Erna went away, I called Mrs. Bailey and told her what had happened and that I had a new guardian, and she said she wouldn't do nothing about changing anything where the kids were concerned long as my new guardian and I got down there before the month was out. I had put away a little money, so I could go without a check for a couple of weeks, and at the beginning of my expecting Jim to be nice I didn't feel too pushy about it. But when the two weeks went by and my money was getting low and the danger of their taking the kids away was getting high, I started really trying to pin him down, and that's when he got mad. We was up in my room, laying on the bed, and the kids were sleeping so it was a crazy fight, all in whispers, but that didn't make it any less hurtful.

"Now, look, Ossie," Jim said, as soon as I brought it up, "it ain't that I don't want to do it, it's that I can't."

I couldn't believe my ears. How could he say that he wasn't going to now that I had told Mrs. Bailey the truth?

"What do you mean, you can't? You told me you'd do it, and I told the worker, and if you don't they'll come and take my kids away!"

Jim got up and sat on the edge of the bed. He reached out his hand and tried to put it on my shoulder, but I shrugged it off.

"You're getting all fussed over nothing," he said, trying to calm me, "and it ain't all like you say. If you just ain't around when they come looking for you, then they can't take your kids, and besides, unless you get in some trouble, I don't think they'd bother, anyhow. Besides, you shouldn't have told that Mrs. Bailey anything. I never did say I could be a guardian, leastwise not straight out, did I?"

I shook my head. It was true that he hadn't said it, but he had let me go on believing he was going to do it, and that was even worse than saying no. When I said that to him he didn't hardly answer me and then what he did say was so low I wasn't sure I heard right.

"I'd do it if I could, but they wouldn't let me be no guardian, even if I tried. I was in some trouble a while back, bad trouble."

I wasn't really listening, or I suppose I would have heard the pain in his voice. All I did hear was no, I ain't gonna help you, and it drove me to a frenzy. I forgot the sleeping kids, I forgot how I had felt about Jim, I just knew I was in big trouble and it was all his fault. I jumped up off the bed, hollering.

"Erna was right! She told me you wasn't going to do it! Sure, as long as you had a nice place to come to and a woman who'd lay for you and nothing asked in return, that was fine, wasn't it? Well, it ain't like that any more, and you can just pick yourself up and get out of here. I don't need you, I'll manage some other way. I always have before and I will again, and I ain't gonna never expect no man to help me, not ever agin. Now git!"

He stood up. "Ain't no use trying to talk to you when you like this. I'll come by, tomorrow or the next day, and we'll figure something out."

I glared at him. "Never you mind. You get out now, and you stay out. I don't need you, and I don't want you no more. You go back and set with your wife and the both of you can rot, setting there just worrying about yourself!"

He didn't say nothing else. He just got up and walked to the door, and he went through it and closed it quiet, and I sat down on the edge of the bed and started trying to figure out what to do.

·14·

I was ignorant, i was young, i was broke, and i was frightened, so I did the only thing all those feelings added up to . . . I ran. I figured I didn't stand a chance of keeping the kids if the welfare caught up with me, and if I stayed in the neighborhood and they came looking, they'd find me, so I packed up the little stuff we had and, with Anthony in my arms and Jackie and Kim clinging to my skirt, got on the bus and rode over to The Other Side of the Hill, back where I started from. When we got down off the bus and I looked around, it was pretty much the way I remembered it, shack and all, but when I started going up and down the streets looking for a room to rent, I saw that the Italians wasn't there any more, leastwise not enough to mention. Almost all the faces were black. Without really thinking about it, I just naturally walked to the house that used to be Aunt Mary's, and when I got there I stood still and looked at it, remembering how it felt to be part of a family, with somebody to watch out for me. I guess I must have looked pretty sad, 'cause a lady who was hanging out wash in the next yard put down her basket and came up to me, asking if I needed help. I told her me and the kids were

138

looking for a place to live, and she said her cousin was fixing to take in somebody and if I went over there I could probably move in right away. She directed me to a street about three blocks away, and we walked over there. The address she gave me was another shack like all the rest, but it had one more room, which meant that it had three, and in those three rooms, when Jackie, Kim, Anthony, and I moved in, were fifteen people, thirteen of them kids. Lila, the lady of the house, was a widow with ten kids, and the only income she had was a small pension, so she needed my fifteen dollars for room, board, and child care pretty bad. It wasn't the place I would have chosen if I'd had a choice, but it did have one plus. I figured the welfare wouldn't even notice Jackie, Kim, Anthony, and me as long as there were so many other kids around. The room I shared with the kids looked pretty much the same as the one I shared with Janet back when we were very little and there was the same walk through the dark to the outhouse, and I thought to myself that I hadn't made much progress with all my scrambling, but we were all still alive and I guess that's what it's all about.

Lila was a good woman, but so wore out that you couldn't even really tell what she looked like. Everything about her drooped, from the wrinkles on her face, to her breasts, to her stockings, to her spirits, but for all that, she kept on trying to stay alive and bring up her kids decent, and you can't ask more than that from any woman. It didn't take my kids hardly any time to get used to living some place new, because there were so many kids in the house, and when kids live with other kids, it's like they're at home right away.

Getting to work from The Other Side of the Hill took about an hour longer than from where I lived before, and sometimes it seemed to me there wasn't nothing left in the world but work and riding that bus. I was beginning to get that rotten, tired feeling again, and when I began feeling that way I remembered that I hadn't gotten my monthly in a while. I put the two things together and came to the conclusion that I was going to have a baby, and for the first time in my life I really didn't want to. It was all I could do to get by with the three I had, but there was never no question in my mind that my having another baby was God's will, so I figured I'd make do some way. I was real scared at the idea of going to the county to have the baby, on account of them wanting to take my kids away, but I figured they had so many people to keep track of that they might have given up on me by the time I had to go there.

I went to live with Lila in September, when the weather was still warm, so things wasn't so bad, but when winter started blowing cold air on that shack being inside it didn't seem to make a lot of difference. There were so many cracks in the old wood that the air just kept coming in even though everything was closed up tight, and the only heat was the coal stove, and that was in the kitchen. When we all went to bed at night, we had on as many clothes as when we were going out, and I sometimes had the crazy feeling that it was warmer outside than in that house. Jackie, Kim, Anthony, and I all slept in one bed, which helped some, 'cause we kind of warmed each other, but when morning came and we had to get up and go outside to the toilet, it was really awful. I was worrying some about Kim, too, 'cause she had a cough that she couldn't seem to lose, no matter what I gave her. I brought home honey from the cafeteria and gave it to her in hot tea, and that seemed to soothe her some, but it didn't last, and I kept telling myself I'd take her to the county if she didn't get better, but I was so afraid to let them get close to my kids that I kept putting it off.

I figured I'd have the baby sometime along about March, and I asked Lila if I could stay and not pay for the time I couldn't work. I knew it was terrible hard on her, but I didn't know what else to do. She understood how I felt about trying to keep my kids with me, and I guess she figured things were so bad anyhow that a few more people wouldn't make much difference, so she said it would be okay. It bothered me to put the extra burden on her, so I did the only thing I could do about it, and it was something I never done before or since. I started taking as much stuff home with me from the cafeteria as I could get without them noticing, things that wouldn't spoil like sugar and flour and cans of beans and such. In a way, I became a one-woman John Clark truck. I know it was wrong, but there didn't seem to be any other way, so I did it.

Every once in a while we had a treat. Lila had a brother named Nero, a big, flashy man who didn't work none that I could see but managed to have sharp clothes and lots of money in his pocket. It puzzled me some that he didn't help Lila much, but I figured it wasn't none of my business, and one thing I will say—when he came around he always brought things for the kids and a big bag of good things to eat. Lila thought the sun rose and set in him, but she wasn't a silly woman and she saw him the way he was. I know, because one night she started telling me how she had practically brought him up after their parents died, her being nine years older than him, and how he was so sweet sometimes and then so mean at other times.

"He's a gambling man," she explained, "and gambling men're very often like that. That's how come he so generous and all. Folks who gamble, seems like they set such store on money, an' then they can't get rid of it fast enough, once they get some. He's a real smart man, too, but he don' seem to want to even try anything else . . . jus' lives it up when he can an' drinks it up when he can't. I seen the way he looked at you tonight. He likes you, but he ain't going to do nothing about it till you have that baby." She laughed. "You ain't his style right now. All his women, they really built."

I knew he had been looking at me, too, but the way I felt, it would be a cold day in August before I got mixed up with any man again. As far as I could see, men like John or my grandfather were mighty scarce, and the kind that weren't scarce were poisonous. They made you feel good for a little while, and then when you needed them they kind of folded up and said they'd like to help you, but they couldn't, or they lit out and you never heard from them again. One thing I did like about Nero, though. He didn't promise nothing, so he couldn't hurt you much. You went with him, you went just for fun. He was right, though. I wasn't built for fun right then. Seems like each time I was expecting I got bigger than the last time, and this time I was so round I waddled when I

walked. It was the best way to look, though, as far as keeping
my job was concerned. The cafeteria never cared whether I
was pregnant, as long as it didn't show too much, 'cause I
guess it made the customers uncomfortable to see a woman
who was expecting a baby toting around heavy trays of dirty
dishes. The way I looked, though, I was just fat, so that was
okay.

Sometime around the middle of February the weather,
which had been bitchy mean up to then, suddenly changed,
and everybody thought spring had come. It wasn't so cold,
and the sun was shining bright, and even the mornings, when
we had to go outside to the toilet, weren't as painful. The kids,
who had been cooped up so much, couldn't get enough of the
outdoors, and they ran wild. It wouldn't have worried me
none, except for Kim, 'cause I knew she wasn't right, and I
didn't want her suddenly taking off her coat in the sunshine
and then getting a chill. I told Lila about it, and she promised
to watch over Kim special, but with all those kids it was pretty
hard. I don't know if it was the change in the weather or if
I'd figured wrong, but four weeks before I figured on having
the baby, I was took with labor pains. I was on the bus coming
home from work, and the pains wasn't little ones like you get
at the beginning, they were real birth pains. I doubled up,
and the driver saw me and stopped the bus. He called a policeman, and the policeman called the county, and the next thing
I knew I was in an ambulance on the way to the hospital. In
between pains I kept trying to tell the ambulance doctor about
letting Lila know where I was, but she didn't have no phone
and could only be reached by calling Nero, and he wasn't
hardly ever home, and the doctor wasn't listening anyhow; and
then, they give me something and I went to sleep. I kind of
woke up when they took me out of the ambulance and then
again in the delivery room, but I didn't really come wide
awake until I'd had the baby and was back in the ward. A
nurse was standing next to me saying, "Okay, Ossie, wake up.
It's all over and you have a fine boy. Open your eyes, now,
c'mon."

I was glad about it being over and about having another
boy and all, but all I could think about was my other kids and

Lila and how they wouldn't know what had happened to me. I told the nurse, and she said not to worry, she'd see that somebody'd call Nero's number until they got him, and she sounded like she'd really take care of it, so I went back to sleep. Turned out she didn't have to do it, though, 'cause Nero was over to Lila's, and when I didn't come home he figured out where I was and called the county, and they told him about me and the baby. When I heard that, my mind was at rest and I began to really enjoy laying in bed and not having to worry about anything for a little while.

I named the new baby James, after his daddy. I knew he'd never be likely to see him, but it seemed like it was the right thing to do, anyhow. He was a pretty small baby, but not scrawny like some, and right from the beginning he was calm. When they'd bring him in to nurse, he just ate and slept and woke up to eat again, and the nurse told me he was the best baby in the nursery. I sure hoped, for his sake, he'd stay that way, 'cause the things you have to face in life ain't so bad if you can keep a grip on them, and calm people seem better able than most to do that.

I didn't expect Lila to drop everything and run over, but by the third day, when she hadn't even called, I began to get mad. After all, when you have a baby, you like to have at least one familiar face come to see you, and besides, before I came to the hospital she used to say she'd visit me when my time came. When visiting hours came around on the afternoon of the fourth day, I kept looking for her and there wasn't no sign. Then, when I'd just about given up, not Lila but Nero walked into the ward. I could see him, way up at the other end, looking for my bed, and I started waving to him. He saw me right off, but he didn't hurry none, and the look on his face kind of put me off. He came and stood at the foot of my bed and he said, "Ossie, all the way over here, I tried to think of a way to tell you what I got to tell you, but there ain't no way that ain't going to hurt. It's about Kim. She's terrible sick, so sick that the doctor says she's like to die."

I guess I must have looked as dazed as I felt. I had heard what he said, but it was so unexpected, so different than the congratulations and jokes I expected that my mind just didn't take it in. He saw it in my face, and he came around the bed and took my hand.

"Maybe I could have led up to it, but I didn't see no point. You a strong gal, and I figured you could stand what you had to, and you got to be ready to stand this."

"I got to see her!"

All I could think of was getting out of that bed and going back to Lila's, to Kim. I knew I wouldn't let her die, that I had to be there with her and save her. Gently, Nero pushed me back into the bed.

"You just set. She right here in this hospital, down to the children's floor. I come down in the ambulance with her, and Lila, she'll be here as soon as she gets a neighbor to watch the kids."

All I really heard was the part about her being in the hospital. I was already on my feet, struggling into the robe the hospital supplied.

A nurse a couple of beds up saw me and came over.

"Going for a walk?" she inquired, with a bright smile.

"Yeh," Nero said. If I'd had any sense, I'd have smiled too, and she would have gone away, but I was too upset to have any sense, and the nurse noticed it.

"Is anything wrong? Perhaps you shouldn't be standing. Maybe you better put off your walk until later, when your husband comes back again."

I just shook my head and started toward the end of the ward.

"Now, just a minute." The nurse laid a hand on my arm. "If there's something you want, I'll get it for you. You're obviously in no condition to . . ."

I shook her off.

"Leave me alone!" My voice was shaking. "I got to go to my baby. She's dying."

"Nonsense! All the babies in the nursery are just fine."

"She don't mean that," Nero said. "It's her little girl, down to the children's floor. I just rode in with her in the ambulance."

The nurse's face changed. She put her arm around me, and gently pushed me back toward my bed.

"You stay here, just one minute, okay? I'll get the supervisor, and we'll get you a wheelchair."

She turned to Nero.

"Please see that she does as I say. I'll be right back. What is the child's name?"

Nero told her, and she walked away quickly.

"Please," I pleaded, "let's go. I don't need no wheelchair, I just need to see Kim."

Before he could answer me, the nurse came back with another one, but not with no wheelchair.

"Now, see here, Mrs. White," the supervisor's voice was kind but very firm. "We understand how you feel, but you can't possibly leave the floor. We'll see to it that you are kept informed about your little girl, and now that she is in capable hands you may rest assured that everything possible is being done for her, and it won't help her to have you become overwrought. Not only are you not in any condition to go to her, but also our rules are very clear about the maternity floor. Once you go to the children's floor, you may not return here nor may you touch your baby, and he needs you. Doctor can care for your little girl, but only you can nurse your new baby. I'll have a phone put next to your bed and . . ."

I was feeling pretty weak and too tired to fight, and the tears started to roll down my cheeks. All at once a feeling that I never remembered having before rolled over me in great big waves, and that feeling was hopelessness. I could fight not ever having enough money, and I could fight the county wanting to break me away from my kids, and I could fight being black and letting the white folks try to make me think black, but I couldn't fight all that and fight the Lord, too. If what I was doing wasn't enough to protect my kids, then what was I doing it for? Things started waving and shimmering, and I guess I kind of slumped, 'cause the nurse and Nero each grabbed for me and lifted me back into the bed.

"Let's let her rest," I heard the supervisor whisper to Nero. "If she sleeps for a while, she'll wake up stronger."

"You gonna get her the phone, like you said?" Nero really wasn't asking. He was telling.

"Of course. We'll do it right away. When you come back

this evening she'll be feeling better, and the phone will be right
there on the table."

The weakness must have put me to sleep, and when I woke
up it was beginning to get dark outside the ward window. As
soon as I opened my eyes I saw the phone standing there just
like the nurse had promised, and, like it was just waiting for
me to wake up, it rang. It was Lila down on the children's
floor with Kim, down where I needed to be and couldn't.

I could tell right away from Lila's voice that things wasn't
no better.

"The doctor says she's holding her own," Lila assured me.
"He says that's as good as it can be right now."

"Is she calling for me?" That seemed to be all I could think
about—Kim, with her sweet little face, wanting her mama and
me not being there.

There was a silence.

"She . . . she ain't exactly awake," Lila said.

"You mean she's unconscious?" I could feel my skin get
cold with fear.

"Nero wants to talk to you." I could hear the relief in
Lila's voice as she handed the phone over to her brother.

"Ossie, now listen." Nero's deep voice was very steady.
"Kim's in a coma. She don't know whether you here or not,
and the one she really needs, the doctor, he's right here now.
He says if she gets through the next few hours, she'll likely be
all right. Lila's got to go home to the rest of the kids, but I'm
gonna stay right here so's I can tell you everything that's going
on. Ain't nothing you could do by being here that you can't
do staying where you are. I promise I'll call you the minute
there's anything new."

I hung up feeling just like I had before I went to sleep. It
was too big for me, too much, and even though Nero said
there wasn't nothing I could do for Kim, somehow I couldn't
stop feeling that if I was there with her I could hold on to her,
like I done before, hold on to her and keep anybody from
taking her away, even the Lord.

I guess maybe when you're tired out and you're weak, you
think things you wouldn't if you didn't feel so poorly, and

maybe that's why, even while I was praying that Kim would be all right, I was sure she'd die and it would be all my fault. The county was right; I wasn't no fit mama to my kids, and now the Lord was going to make me see it, if the county couldn't. It was pride that made me think I could work and take care of the kids proper, pride and a feeling that I could show my own mama that it could be done, that I didn't have to leave Jackie and Kim and Anthony like she had left me and Alice and the rest of us. The Lord didn't hold much with pride, at least pride that ain't got no reason to be there, and like it said in the Bible, pride goeth before a fall, and I was falling.

I almost held my breath, waiting for that phone to ring, and when about an hour later it did, I knew before I answered what I was going to hear.

"Ossie," Nero's voice wasn't so steady now.

"She's gone, ain't she?" I didn't even have to ask the question. I knew.

"She's gone, but she didn't suffer at all. She never woke up or anything, just went to sleep and stayed asleep. You got to think maybe she's luckier than we all are. Being alive, when you're black, it ain't so much. She never had to find that out."

I guess I hung up. I don't remember doing it. A few minutes later Nero came to the ward, and I could see him talking to the nurse down by her desk. She got right up and came over to my bed and started getting busy with a needle.

"I heard about your little girl," she said, holding the needle and looking at it. "I've brought you something that will help you sleep and gather your strength."

"I don't need to gather no strength." It was my voice, and it was me talking, but I felt so funny, like there was two of me. "I gotta stay awake, like the Lord says, stay awake and feel the pain. Otherwise, why did Kim die?"

"You don't know what you're saying," she said, rubbing my arm with something. "You've had a shock, when you aren't well enough to roll with it, and that's why you feel the way you do, but you'll get over it. I'm giving you something to help you, so don't fight it. Just close your eyes."

I closed them, like she said, and the minute I did I saw Kim's face and heard her little voice calling, "Mama, Mama, Mama," and a pain like a deep cut started between my breasts and ran up my neck and down my arms and brought me sitting up straight in my bed. I suppose I must have looked as wild as I felt, and the nurse jammed the needle in my arm and then stood there, holding my hand and saying things about how everything passes and this would pass too. She pushed me gently down on the pillow, and slowly her face and her voice and the pain all faded away.

· 15 ·

THAT NURSE WAS RIGHT, AND SHE WAS WRONG. TIME PASSED, like she said, and I got stronger and was able to leave the hospital, but the pain didn't pass, except that *it* got stronger, too, and left the hospital right with me. They said I was too sick to go to Kim's funeral, and I let them tell me that 'cause I didn't think I could stand it, and then that was one more thing to add to the things I didn't do for Kim. Nero paid for the burying and Lila comforted Jackie and Anthony, and I just woke up in the morning, breathed all day so's I wouldn't die, and went to sleep at night, hardly being able to wait to do it and hoping I wouldn't wake up in the morning. I knew I would, though, 'cause the Lord wasn't going to let me escape the pain that easy.

I guess I'd have been better off without Lila and Nero then, 'cause I'd have had to pull myself together and go back to work, but all the push was out of me, and as long as Lila was willing to have me stay, I didn't ask no questions. Nero was around a lot more than he had been before, and he was helping with the money, and I knew I should have let him know I was grateful, but the effort of talking was too much, and I just kind of sat and let things go. It seemed like I didn't have no strength left over for anything, 'cause I was using it all up just living with that pain. Lucky for Jackie and Anthony, the house was so full of kids they wasn't lonely, and James was too young to care about anything but getting fed and sleeping.

For a while Nero just left me alone, waiting for me to come back to life, but after a few weeks I guess he decided I wasn't going to do it by myself. He took to showing up after the evening meal dressed in his best and on his way to wherever it was he went and trying to talk me into going along. At first I didn't even bother to make up excuses, just said no, but he took to getting mad or at least putting on that he was, and then finally he started saying how he did for me when I needed him and now he needed me and I was turning him down. One night when he was pushing me to go get dressed and come along, I asked him what it was he needed me for. I didn't believe him, just figured he was saying that because he thought it would get to me, and I didn't expect him to have no reasonable answer, but he did.

"I got me a new bunch of friends," he said, "real nice people who go out with their wives and their girlfriends of an evening, looking for a little excitement. Now, I know where the excitement is, and if I was going to be along with *my* girl when they all go out, I could just mention, kinda cool, that I'd heard about a place where we could all have a good time, and then I wouldn't be no shill, just one of the bunch trying to have a good time. And it ain't like I'm expecting you to do anything. I just want you to get dressed and come along and be nice, that's all."

"Why me?" I asked. "You probably know plenty of girls who'd like to go with you, girls a lot prettier than me and with better clothes, too."

Nero looked disgusted.

"For a smart gal, you sure ask dumb questions. I got my reasons, that's all. Would I be sitting here bothering with you if I didn't have my reasons? I didn't ask you no dumb questions when you was in trouble, did I?"

I suppose he knew that was the only way to pull me out

of the house, and it worked. He had been good to me and I owed him, so I went and got dressed, but when I got back in the kitchen Nero really got mad.

"You think I'm taking you out to meet my friends looking like that? Where's your make-up? How come you didn't comb your hair? You ain't so pretty you can look good just any old way, you know."

Stung, I marched back to my room. Nobody was going to tell *me* I didn't look good enough to go out with him. I did everything I could think of to make myself look as attractive as possible, and it must have helped, 'cause this time when I went back in the kitchen, although Nero didn't fall over in no dead faint 'cause I was so gorgeous, he did admit that I looked better.

"Okay," he said, "now all you gotta do is be nice. Don't look surprised at anything I say, and don't talk too much. I got a car outside; it ain't mine, but they gonna think it is, and we're going to pick them up in it. You is the gal I'm gonna marry, and you ain't got no troubles and you ain't got no kids, and you kinda dumb. You just keep your eyes and ears open and follow my lead and you be fine." He grinned suddenly. "Come to think of it, the way you been acting, playing dumb ain't gonna be no chore at all."

It was like he said. In his borrowed car, which was a nice new Buick, we rode over to Madisonville, where black people who could afford to live like white people had their homes. We stopped in front of a new up-and-downstairs house, and Nero said he'd go get his friends while I waited in the car. The excitement and the change had kind of pulled me together, but as soon as he got out and left me alone, the pain started at me again and all I wanted to do was run home, back where I could hide. The pain was so strong, and it pulled so hard, that I broke out in a cold sweat and grabbed on to the handle of the door just so's I wouldn't get out and run, and I sat there shaking, telling myself that Nero had been good to me and I couldn't run off and leave him in the lurch, and praying he'd come back soon, 'cause I didn't know how long I could hold out. In what was probably a couple of minutes but seemed like a couple of years, the big door to the house opened and Nero came out with two men and two women. They was all dressed to the teeth and talking and laughing, and they come toward the car like Nero was waving them on to do. He come up next to the door where I was sitting and he opened it and said to all of them, "This here's Ossie, the gal who's gonna be my wife. Ossie, meet Fred and June and Gene and Rosalie, the friends I was telling you about."

They all piled into the car. Gene, a big light-colored man, pushed in next to me on the front seat, and the other three sat in the back, and we was off.

"I can't wait to see this place," one of the girls in the back said, with a giggle. "I've never been in a gambling house before. Does it look like they do in the movies, Nero?"

"How should I know?" Nero, who was busy driving, seemed to find the question silly. "I never been there before. I told Gene here that I just heard about it from a fella at work, and he said he had a good time, so I figured I'd try it. We don't like it, we can always split."

"You like to gamble, Ossie?" Gene was sitting next to me, and he asked the question to cover up the fact that he was rubbing his big thigh against me, knowing there wasn't no room for me to move away.

"I reckon." Nero said I should play dumb, and I didn't feel like talking anyhow, and if I had felt like talking I wouldn't have picked nobody who wanted to rub me before he even decently knew my name.

Nero laughed. "That's Ossie for you. She ain't never gambled in her life, but she's ready to try anything, ain't you, girl?"

This time I just nodded.

"She doesn't say much, does she?" Gene said, as if I wasn't even there.

"No, she don't," Nero chuckled, "but she thinks a lot."

"And I pinch, too." I said it so low that only Gene could hear me, and I guess he did, 'cause from then on he kept his leg still.

Pretty soon Fred, in the back, noticed the direction we was going in.

"You're not driving to The Other Side of the Hill, are you, Nero?"

Nero nodded.

"Do you think it's okay to take the girls there?" Fred's voice was uncertain.

"Why not?" his girl, June, demanded. "After all, it's not like we're alone. I mean, okay, three girls alone wouldn't go there, but with you fellows along, what can happen to us?"

I know what can happen to me, I thought. I can go home and go to bed.

"Well, I hope you know what you're doing." Fred still didn't sound happy. "There are some pretty rough characters hanging out around that slum. Those people don't even act civilized half the time."

I stole a look at Nero and I could see he was having a real good time. He was enjoying what Fred was saying, but I was getting mad. What he said and the way he said it reminded me of my sister Alice, and I was thinking that even though I hadn't seen her in a long time and I didn't rightly know how she'd turned out, I'd bet my life on her bein' a holier-than-thou shit-ass like Fred seemed to be.

"Oh, come on, Fred." Rosalie, who hadn't said anything up to now, sounded annoyed. "You know better than that. You're just saying that because you're afraid somebody'll think you're the same as they are. Don't worry, we all know you, and we know you wouldn't be caught dead acting like an uncivilized African."

"Damn it, you know that's not what I mean!" I figured she must have hit him where it hurt, 'cause he sounded so mad. "Lord spare me from psych majors. In a rough neighborhood like we're going to, they'd just as soon cut you up as look at you, and you know it, and they don't even think they're doing anything wrong!"

"Just calm down," Nero said soothingly. "My friend says this place is nice and civilized and safe. Nobody carries knives

or razors, and they all act like gentlemen. They cheat and lie
and steal, always nonviolently, of course."

Everybody in the car thought that was pretty funny, and I
looked at Nero with new eyes. He was smarter than I thought,
and he could act better than half the men I saw in the movies.
I began to feel a little better, although I still wanted to go
home.

We rode a couple of minutes more, and then Nero pulled up
in front of one of the few fairly decent houses on The Other
Side of the Hill. We all got out and waited by the front door
while Nero said something in a low tone to the big man who
opened it, and then we was all allowed to go inside. The front
room looked just like any other front room, but then we went
through a door into what I figured would be the dining room,
and it wasn't like no dining room I ever saw. They must have
made two rooms into one, 'cause it was so big and it was full
of tables—crap tables and twenty-one tables and the like—
and there was some people standing around playing or watching. There was a window with bars on it, and behind it a man
in a green eye shade who handed out chips and took in money.
Nero kind of herded us all over to the barred window, and
everybody started reaching for their money so's they could
buy chips. I figured I'd like to try a little myself, but Nero
put his hand on my arm and shook his head a little bit, so I just
stood there. When everybody had got their chips, Nero went
to the window, and I noticed that he got chips but he didn't
give no money for them. He gave a few to me and told me
to enjoy myself, and then he kind of wandered off.

I just walked around for a while, watching. Most of the
folks who was gambling were black, but there were a few
whites mixed in, and all of them was pretty well dressed and,
like Nero said, quiet and well behaved. Once in a while somebody would get hot at the crap table, and then everybody
would gather 'round and there'd be a little cheering, but other
than that there was just a kind of low hum. I could see the
other four people we came with gambling or watching, but
there wasn't no sign of Nero. For a while I didn't mind,
'cause it was kind of interesting, and besides, the man at the

twenty-one table showed me how to play, and I even won a little, but then I began getting itchy to leave and I wanted to know where Nero had got to. I walked all around and he wasn't no place in that room, and I didn't want to ask the other four if they had seen him, 'cause I had a feeling he wouldn't like that, so finally I just give up and sat down and waited. Sitting like that, the pain began to get to me again and I closed my eyes and tried not to feel it, and pretty soon I heard Nero's voice, right behind me and kind of low.

"Don't go drifting off, girl. I just won a piece of the world for us." He come around in front of me, grinning the biggest grin I ever saw on him.

"Where'd you go off to?" I demanded. "I couldn't find you nowhere!"

"Back there." He pointed behind me, but when I turned all I saw was a blank wall. "There's a door back there. You can't see it less'n you know it's there. That's where the real playing goes on. This here's just for suckers, ladees and gent'muns like our friends." The contempt he felt for the people he called his "friends" was written all over his face. "That's where the real people hang out, the guys who aren't afraid to be alive."

"You mean this kind of gambling ain't the kind you do?" I waved my hand in the direction of the tables.

"You bet your sweet life it ain't. These cats, they all suckers. Ain't got a chance, not a chance in a million. Back there, they don't shoot craps and they don't play twenty-one. They just sit and play a nice quiet game of poker, and that's a game where what you are counts as much as what you got. Can't nobody with a weak gut sit in *that* game, you can bet on it."

"Well, if that's what you come for, how come you bothered to bring these other people, and how come it mattered if I came?"

"'Cause I get paid for it," Nero said. "I try to meet folks who got enough money to come here and lose some of it and not get tight about what happens, and every time I bring a few, I get part of a stack of chips. I let the chips sit for a couple of times and then I get enough to stake me in the poker game. If I lose, it ain't all out of my pocket, in a manner of

speaking, and if I win . . . well, it's worth counting, and tonight I won."

"Then can we go home?" All of a sudden I was so tired I
thought I was going to go right through the floor, and I could
feel the tears starting to push at my eyeballs. Nero looked at
me, close.

"You done real good for the first time," he said. "Soon's we
can get them squares all together, we'll take 'em back where
they come from, and then we'll go on home, okay?"

Nero was as good as his word. He kinda herded the other
four out into the car without being too pushy about it, and
when they all said they wanted to go some place and eat he
said he had an early day coming up and he'd drop them home
and then they could do as they pleased. He sounded so much
like a big businessman that even I believed him, and after he
dropped the four of them off I just slid down in my seat and
kinda drifted off, 'cause I knew I didn't have to pretend any
more.

"You really want to go home?"

I opened my eyes, surprised. "Sure I do. Where else would I
want to go?"

"Well, you ain't never seen where I live."

Wearily, I shook my head. "And I ain't going to, not tonight I ain't. It ain't that I don't want to, it's that I can't. All
the time now, I feel like I'm half dead and I'd rather feel like
that than have the pain."

"You feel like you're half dead because you are, and if you
go on letting yourself do like you're doing, you ain't never
going to be any different. I could *really* make you feel much
better, and keep you feeling that way."

"No you couldn't," I answered. "Ain't nobody or nothing
can do that. You could make the pain go away for a minute,
but it would sit right there, waiting to come back, so what's
the use?"

"I think you want that pain, 'cause when you're feeling it
you think you're making up to Kim. And besides, if I can
make you not feel it for a little while, what's wrong with that?
Unless you wanta feel it all the time, like I said."

I realized the car wasn't rolling any more.

"This here's my place." Nero pointed to a rooming house about three doors down from where we was parked. "You say yes, we go in, you say no, I take you home. It's up to you."

Like everything else just then, it was too much trouble to make up my mind. I didn't say anything.

"That mean you staying?" Nero sounded like he didn't really care either way.

I nodded my head. "I'll stay, but you gonna be disappointed. If I'm really half dead, like you say, can't nobody bring me back."

"Honey," said Nero, "there ain't nothin I can't do tonight."

·16·

THAT'S HOW IT STARTED, MY BEING NERO'S PARTNER. I WASN'T really, but that's what he called me, 'cause he knew I felt better about taking money from him that way. At the beginnning he just kind of pulled me along with him, and with me feeling the way I did, it was a relief having somebody tell me what to do and when to do it. He treated me real good, and he treated the kids real good, and when we was in bed together he knew how to make me feel like a woman again and, best of all, he didn't promise me nothing, so I wasn't scared to begin feeling again.

Like I said, Lila thought the sun rose and set in him, but she kept kinda warning me not to get too mixed up with him, and I kept telling her not to worry about it—nobody was pulling any wool over my eyes, I knew what I was doing. Whenever I said that, she used to look at me like she wanted to say something else, but then she didn't say it. Later on I found out how smart she had been. She knew I wouldn't believe her until I saw it for myself, so she wasn't really protecting me against anything, and she knew I'd just get mad at her besides.

Nero had been on a winning streak. He knew it and I

knew it, but of course we never mentioned it, 'cause he taught me right away that there are things gamblers don't talk about, and good luck is the most important. I got used to going out with him and his "friends," and even got to enjoying it, and he bought me some real good-looking clothes, and we went out to nice places, and I began to feel like my worst times were over. I didn't believe it down deep, 'cause I had gotten to a place where you never believe anything like that for sure, but at least I *did* feel like I was a person and not a thing.

The first time he lost after we took up together, I guess he just figured it was to be expected, 'cause, as he told me, you can't win 'em all. Sure enough, the next time he won again, and the time after that. He called me his rabbit's foot, and started being superstitious about me, too, like refusing to gamble at all any more unless I was somewhere in hailing distance. This got to be kinda tough on me, 'cause now I had to go with him even when he wasn't herding any "friends," and sometimes, when he was playing poker, there wasn't no place for me to wait where I could even rightly sit down, so I'd have to wait outside in the car he had bought. It got very tiresome, just sitting, but he wouldn't have it no other way, and I found out that while he was mostly agreeable, when it came down to something he really wanted there wasn't nothing could change his mind.

I didn't like going along all the time, but I figured it was the least I could do, seeing as how he was so good to me in so many ways, and that's the way it was. Lucky for me, I could fall asleep any place, anyhow, and I spent a lot of time curled up on the seat of the car, dead to the world. Sometimes when I woke up my legs wouldn't wake up with me and I'd have to kind of crawl out and walk around until I got them feeling like legs again, and that's what I was doing the night Nero went for a bundle. It was about four o'clock in the morning, and it was on a street in Walnut Hill that was pretty dark to start with, and at that time of the morning was pitch black. I woke up 'cause I thought I heard a door slam, but I must have been dreaming, and then I noticed how I was aching all over from being so cramped for so long, so I got out of the car and started walking up the block. I wasn't no more than half a block away when I heard Nero's voice yelling, "Ossie! Where you at? You dumb black bitch, where you got to? Ossie! If I find you, I'm gonna lay you out!"

I never heard him sound like that before, and I never heard him so mad before, and I didn't know what to do. Part of me figured I ought to hide, but another part didn't believe he meant what he was saying, and after all, it was Nero, my friend Nero who'd been so good to me. I started up the block toward him, not walking real fast, but kind of wanting to get close enough to see if he looked as mad as he sounded and, rotten luck for me, he saw me before I saw him. With a roar, he leaped out of the dark and caught hold of my arms, twisting them behind me, and then, holding both my hands in one of his, he started hitting me in the face with the other. He was doing it in a kind of back-and-forth rhythm and saying through gritted teeth, "Run out on me, will you? I'll teach you to run, you raunchy bitch. They ain't never got me down, and you ain't gonna help 'em . . . I'll fix you!"

I kept opening my mouth trying to scream, but the slaps was taking my breath away. Suddenly he let go of my hands and grabbed me by the shoulders and started pushing and pulling me, away from him and back to him, and hard, so's every time he slammed me back at him my body hit him like he was a brick wall. I couldn't hardly breathe and things was beginning to get kind of far away and my knees was sagging, and then he threw me in the back of the car. I was too far gone to do anything but lay there, and I could hear him breathing like he was gonna choke as he went around to the driver's side, slammed into the front seat, and started the motor.

I knew he was drunk, I could smell it, and I wanted to jump out, but nothing was working right, and there wasn't nothing I could do but lay there and pray. From the way the car was swaying I figured he must be driving pretty fast, and I kept expecting to crash into something, but nothing happened except I just kept getting thrown from side to side. I figured he was driving back to his place, but when the car finally stopped and he started dragging me out, we was in front of Lila's. I was pretty relieved, 'cause I figured she could handle him if I couldn't, and I thought the worst was over, but I was wrong. He was dragging me with one hand and banging on the front door with the other, screaming and cursing at the top of his voice, and I was crying and sobbing and trying to twist free, and we must have been quite a sight.

When Lila opened up, he didn't expect it and he was pounding on the door so hard that when she opened it he fell in, flat on his face, dragging me down half under him and knocking my breath out all the way. I blacked out, but it couldn't have been for long, 'cause when I come to I was still laying on the floor by the door, and Lila and the children was screaming while Nero rampaged through the house, smashing furniture and breaking dishes and destroying everything that he could lay his hands on. I was so close to the front door I figured I could drag myself outside and maybe go for help, so I started crawling on all fours, hoping he wouldn't notice me, and I got halfway out before he threw himself on me and started pounding my head into the door frame. That's when I really went out.

When I come to the next time I was laying on my bed and all the kids was standing around kind of snuffling. Lila had a pan of water and a washcloth and was wiping my face and my head, and every time she took the cloth away, I could see it was red. I had so many pains in so many places that none of them really made any impression, and I figured I was pretty bad off. There was a buzzing in my head and a funny deep moaning and grunting sound that didn't seem to be coming from anywhere, and then Lila put her hand under my head and raised it a little off the pillow so's she could get to the back of my neck with the cloth, and I saw Nero scrunched up in the corner on the floor, crying and making that moaning I heard.

When Lila saw my eyes was open, she put down the basin and sat down on the bed next to me. Then she called all the kids around and told them to look and see how I was all right now. Jackie and Anthony crept up on the bed, and I held tight to their hands for a minute, and then all the kids went outside.

Lila kind of patted my arm and said, "It's all over, thank the Lord, and you'll be all right. You don't look so good, and it'll be a while before them bruises go away, but you'll be all right . . . yes, sirree, you'll be all right now."

"Maybe I'll be all right, but he won't." I pointed at Nero, or at least I tried to, but my arm wasn't working too good. "When he finally get out of jail, he's gonna be too old to be all right."

"Now, now," Lila said calmly, "you don't really mean that. You just hurting and feeling mean, an' I don't blame you none, but tomorrow you feel better and you be talking different."

"I won't be talking different tomorrow or next week or any time! You know what he done . . . you saw what he done . . . and I'll wager you seen it plenty of times before, judging from the fact you ain't surprised this time. Well, he ain't no better than no wild animal, carrying on like that, and wild animals live in cages, and so's he gonna live in a cage . . . and for just as long as they'll keep him. And if they want to let him out, I'll go and tell them how wild he is and they'll put him back."

"Honey, you talking crazy. Sure Nero losing and Nero drinking is a mean cuss, but Nero winning and Nero not drinking is about the kindest man that ever lived, and one of the smartest, too."

"That's crap," I said. "If he was so all-fired smart he wouldn't be no shill for a bunch of cheap crooks, and he wouldn't have to gamble to stay alive, and . . ."

"And he'd be the President of the United States, right?"

"He don't have to be President. He just have to get a job and use those brains of his for something worth doing!" Suddenly all the pains and aches and all the anger and fear came over me in big waves. I didn't want to cry, but I couldn't help it; I just started sobbing and sobbing and I couldn't stop, and when I'd cried till I couldn't cry any more, Lila looked pleased.

"Now," she said, as though we'd settled something important, "now you'll stop wanting to put Nero in a cage, and you'll be able to remember how good he's been to you. If you want to make him feel bad for a while, you go right ahead, 'cause he expects that and he needs it, but you don't go getting the police mixed up in all this, hear?"

She looked at me, waiting for me to agree, but I didn't say nothing. I couldn't forget how frightened I was that Nero would kill not only me but Lila and all the kids.

"How do I know he won't do it again?" I demanded. "And how do I know the next time he won't kill all of us? I know he's your brother and all, but he's crazy mean when he's drinking and he's dangerous."

Lila began to lose patience with me. "Because he *is* my brother. And because, like you said, I seen him this way before, lots of times before, and he ain't killed nobody yet. He slams around until he gets all the mad and hurt out of him, and then he's himself again, like now."

I looked over to the corner of the room. Nero had worn himself out with his moaning, and he was sleeping on the floor, but not a real sleep, 'cause he was twitching something fierce, and his face was all twisted like he was in bad pain. Even though he looked awful, the mean, ugly look was gone, and he looked like the Nero who helped me stay alive, and I could feel myself begin to listen to what Lila was saying.

Like she said, I wasn't going to die, but I *did* look awful for a while. I didn't much like the way I looked, but I figured it didn't really hurt none, because Nero, who was terrible ashamed of himself to start with, kept looking at the bruises and cut marks like they was more than he could stand, and rubbing it in was exactly what I wanted to do. After the first couple of days, when he was so low he didn't even try to talk to anybody, he started trying to explain what made him do what he did, but I wasn't listening, and pretty soon he just covered it over and started to act like nothing ever happened, and in a week or two everything went back to being the way it was before. He wasn't winning all the time, but he wasn't losing big, and he was even nicer and more loving than he had been before he went out of his mind, and pretty soon the whole thing just faded away . . . almost. It faded, too, because I wanted it to. Nero was the only man I ever knew who took care of me enough so's I didn't have to work and I could stay home and take care of my kids, and that made up for an awful lot. I could be a real mother, with time to talk to Jackie and play games with Anthony and cuddle James, and watch them grow and keep them safe.

That's why, about two months after Nero's spell, I figured out I was pregnant again, and I didn't mind. Having kids, when you can stay home and be with them, is about the nicest thing that can happen to a woman, and it looked like this time I was going to be able to do just that. When I told Nero about it, he didn't look real happy, but he didn't carry on, neither, and that was about what I expected. He wasn't no family man, and he never said he was, so that was all right. For the first time in a long time, I just settled down to being a woman the way a woman ought to be, and if it hadn't been for the pain I felt over Kim, I guess I would have been pretty happy. Sometimes, for an hour or two, I could forget her dying all alone, but then right in the middle of feeling good I'd see her face, and it was like a shock went through me and my chest got heavy and I was cold all over, and I could only get warm again by hugging Jackie or the babies. Lila kept saying that when enough time passed I'd forget, or at least not hurt so bad, but I didn't see no signs of that, and I didn't even hope for it.

When I was about six months along, I thought maybe I better go to the county clinic. I figured if they hadn't bothered me about the kids when I was in the hospital the last time, it was safe, so I rode downtown on the bus, meaning to go and talk to a doctor, but I never got there. The bus was going along and I was sitting by the window looking out, and it came to a bus stop and there waiting to get on was my sister Alice. She was dressed real nice, like the girls who lived in Madisonville, and she had her nose up in the air, like she always did, and I wasn't sure I wanted her to see me, but before I could do anything about it she climbed in, looked around, and spotted me right away. She came hurrying up the aisle and sat down next to me and, just like Alice, didn't even say hello, just started right in being snotty.

"I knew some day I'd run into you. Where in hell have you been? Mama's almost crazy trying to find you. If you didn't care about any of the rest of us, you could at least have cared about her enough to let her know where you got to. Of course, I wasn't surprised at the way you acted, knowing how immature you've always been."

Alice always brought out the devil in me, with her being so high-handed. If she had just said hello or I'm glad I found you, I'd have told her everything that happened, and I'd have been glad to get back with my own people again, but because she was the way she was, I just couldn't do it.

I gave her what I hoped was a cold smile. "Nothing to get so excited about. I've been here all the time, and people just naturally lose track of each other sometimes. You look like you having it pretty good."

She smiled that smug smile that used to throw me into a fit when we was kids. "Yes, things have worked out very nicely, like they often do when you plan your life instead of just living from day to day. I see you're expecting a baby. Congratulations."

If we hadn't been in a public place and as old as we were, I think I would have hit her. Instead, I just smiled and said thank you.

"Who's the father? Anybody respectable?"

That did it. The devil took over, and from then on it was him talking, not me.

"You mean the father of this here one, or the other three?"

She wasn't ready for that, and the snooty look on her face went away and she just looked surprised.

"You've got four children?"

I nodded. "Would have had five, but one died." I said it as flat as I could.

She stopped looking like snooty Alice and looked like my sister. "Oh, Ossie, how awful for you. When did it happen?"

"About a year." I wasn't about to let her know how I felt.

People like Alice get nice and you forget how they really are, and later you're sorry. She looked real sad.

"I've been married almost three years and I've never been pregnant, and I want a baby so bad. We could afford one, too, and give it a good home and intelligent care, but so far no luck. Doesn't seem fair, does it, you having all these kids you probably don't even want . . ."

I looked her right in the eye and said, "Maybe I should have tried to let Mama know where I was, but it was worth not seeing her so's I didn't have to see you. Who in hell made you so all-fired high and mighty? What you done to be so proud about?"

She *did* look uncomfortable, I'll say that for her.

"I didn't mean anything wrong," she said. "I know you can't be married again, because you never were divorced from Charles and . . ."

I was so surprised I forgot I was mad. "How come you know about that?"

"That's one of the reasons Mama was looking for you. A few months ago Charles got in touch with her. He couldn't find you and he had met a girl he wanted to marry and he wanted a divorce. Of course, Mama couldn't be much help, but she promised to let him know if she ever found you, so please, even if you don't want to see me again, either tell me where you're living or let me give you Mama's address. And Ossie, I'm sorry. I shouldn't have said what I did. It's only that you always were . . ."

"Why don't you quit now, before you say something else I ain't going to like?"

She smiled, and for a minute I felt close and warm and like I really had found my family again.

I noticed we was getting close to where I had to get off for the clinic and I started getting ready to get up.

"You going some place you have to go right this minute?"

I shook my head.

"Then sit down. I'm on my way to where Mama's living now. Why don't you come along?"

I sat back down, kind of hesitating in my mind. It was so

long since I'd seen my family, and so much had happened to me, and I wasn't sure I wanted to see Mama again with Alice around, but there didn't seem no way out of it. And besides, I *did* want to find out about Charles and the divorce. I guess I must have cared more than I thought about what Mama would think of me, 'cause the closer that bus got to where we was going to get off, the jumpier I got.

When Alice rang the bell to Mama's front door, I kind of edged behind her like I was trying to hide, and even after Mama opened the door and looked real surprised and happy to see me and took me in her arms, I kept feeling like I wanted to run home. Her and Alice told me all about the family, how my brother Verne was in the navy, and Alice had graduated from college and married an electrical engineer, and John was making good money, good enough so's Mama didn't have to work anymore, and Janet was living in New York trying to be an actress . . . and then they sat back and waited for me to tell them all about what I'd been doing. I was going to try, but it was like my tongue stuck in my mouth, and instead I stood up and said I was late for an appointment, and could I please have Charles' address, and I'd see them all soon. They wanted to know where I was living and I said I was moving but I'd let them know my new address as soon as I knew it myself, and as soon as Mama wrote down where to get in touch with Charles, I started for the door.

"Ossie," Mama said, real low so Alice wouldn't hear, "you can tell me where you been and what you done. I won't hold it against you."

I felt such a rush of anger that it almost knocked me off my feet. "I don't care whether you do or don't. What I been doing, I been doing so's I can stay with my kids, and that's good enough for me. I ain't been running off and leaving them like you done."

Mama looked like I hit her across the face. "How come you say something like that? I did what I had to do."

I shook my head. "Didn't look that way to me. Seems like if I could stay with my kids, without even a father for 'em, you could have done it too."

"Mama was trying to make a decent life for us." Suddenly Alice was there in the middle of it, as usual. I put my hand on the door and opened it a little bit.

"That's right," she said. "Run away again, run away and live in the gutters you like to live in. Go on having babies without fathers to care for them and tell yourself you're being a better mother than Mama was. You don't really believe it, though; I can see you don't in your eyes."

"You be quiet!" Mama told Alice fiercely. "This ain't none of your business. You don't know what Ossie been through, and neither do I, so you can't judge."

She looked at me with so much understanding that I wanted to cry, to get down on my knees and beg her to forgive me for what I said to her, but I ain't never been able to act like that and I couldn't then. All I did was try to smile at her, and as I went out the door I said in a low voice, "I'll let you know where I am pretty soon."

Riding home on the bus I kept turning and turning the whole thing over in my mind. I felt uneasy and scared and like I'd come to a new place where I was all alone and lost and had to find my way. Things had happened to me so hard and so fast that I guess I just never thought about them, just did what I thought I had to do and never looked at *why* I did them or how I felt, and now, when I got so mad at Mama, it was like all the feelings I hadn't felt came pouring over me and I like to drown in them. I kept hearing her voice saying about how if you don't know what a person's been through you can't rightly judge them, and I realized I had judged her that way, and it was wrong. By the time I got home I was so worn out you'd have thought I'd walked all the way, and, in my mind, I guess I'd walked even further.

· 17 ·

It turned out the number Mama gave me wasn't Charles himself but a lawyer who was handling the divorce for him. I had to go down to his office to sign some papers, and that was all I knew about it until lots later when I got an official-looking paper saying I wasn't married to Charles any more.

It didn't make no difference to Nero about my getting divorced 'cause he wasn't about to get married anyhow, and even if he'd wanted to I didn't. I was getting near my time, and of course I couldn't go out with him and his "friends" any more and I was tired all the time, so we hardly ever made love. His luck wasn't very good, and he kept grumbling about his rabbit's foot wasn't doing her job, but I guess what kept him from really getting het up was remembering what he done to me before. Lila started looking pretty nervous and telling me that maybe I should force myself to at least go along and sit in the car, but I was too uncomfortable and too big, and besides, I figured he'd start winning again without me along and then I wouldn't be stuck with going with him after the baby was born.

Like usual with me, all hell broke loose at the worst pos-

sible time. I was about a week into my ninth month and having
a lot of sneaky pains that wasn't labor but kept me wondering
if they was. Nero was fed up with having a woman who
wasn't no good to him and was sick besides, but mostly he was
fed up with losing, and he was getting meaner and meaner,
and finally he told me he'd heard about a poker game with
some of the biggest gamblers in the city and he was going to
sit in on it. I didn't say nothing, although I agreed with Lila
when she tried to say that if his luck was bad maybe he ought
to wait till it changed, but she was his sister, and he almost
hit her when she even mentioned it, so I figured I'd better
shut up.

He got all dressed up and left about seven in the evening.
After the kids went to bed, Lila and I played double solitaire
for a while, but I was too uncomfortable to sit for long, so
along about nine I went to bed. I kept falling asleep and
waking up because something hurt me, and then falling asleep
again, until finally it was hard to know which was sleeping
and which was being awake. All of a sudden I heard a lot of
hollering and banging and I started to get up but being so big
I couldn't move very fast, and by the time I got to the bedroom door, in came Nero, drunk, roaring crazy mad, looking
for me, and liquored up enough to kill me dead. Lila came
running after him, begging him to calm down and trying to
grab his arm, and when I saw what she was trying to grab
away from him, I almost fainted. Some place, maybe on his
way to my room, he had gotten a kitchen knife, a long, sharp
carving knife that could cut off anybody's head easy as slicing
a cabbage. The way he was when he was drunk he probably
didn't even know he was holding it, and that made it even
worse. The kids woke up and started to scream, and Jackie
jumped out of bed and came running to me, and by doing that
I think she saved my life. She got between Nero and me and
she was so small he didn't see her and she got tangled up in
his legs and tripped him. He went sprawling on the floor, the
knife flying out of his hand, and he hit the ground with so
much force that he knocked himself out.

Lila and I didn't waste no time talking, we just got all the kids together and ran outside and up to the corner, where a friend of Lila's lived. Just when we got in front of her friend's house, I was taken with a pain that doubled me over, so Lila got her friend's husband to run to a phone to call the county, and they come with the ambulance and took me in. Just before they put me on the stretcher I told Lila my mother's address and asked her if she could get my kids there so's Nero couldn't find them, and she promised she would, and that relieved my mind considerable.

They took me to the county hospital and a couple of hours later Bertie was born. He was the biggest of all my babies, weighing almost nine pounds, and I guess that was because he was the only one I carried when I was taking proper care of myself. Mama came to see me in the hospital and said the kids was fine and that when I got out she wanted us all to stay with her for a while, and it sounded real good to me. Lila came too and said that after Nero come to he felt terrible like last time and begged her to tell him where I was, but she didn't and promised me she never would. I guess she finally knew that he was dangerous when he was liquored up and losing.

I took Bertie back to Mama's like she asked me to, and it felt mighty good to be there. I tried, after I was there a day or two, to apologize for the mean way I had treated her the day I ran into Alice, but she said it was too long ago to even remember, and I guess she meant it, 'cause it never came up again. The kids loved Mama and John right away and they started talking about staying forever, but I told them we couldn't do that. Mama said why not, and I tried to explain that I was so used to living on my own that I couldn't rightly change back now, and although that may have been part of it, it sure wasn't most of it.

I could see that John and Mama had gotten used to being alone together, and it didn't seem right to me to move in with four kids at this stage of the game, so I just let them think I wanted to be moving on once I was strong enough. They tried to talk me out of it, and I think they wanted to mean it, even if they didn't really, but I could see the relief in their eyes when I wouldn't change my mind.

When Bertie was three weeks old, John came home one night and said he'd found a job for me next door to where he worked, doing house work for a very nice lady. It was just what I wanted, 'cause she didn't have no children, so I didn't have to sleep in, and that meant I could find a place for me and the kids and come home to them every night. I was nursing Bertie and figured I'd better wean him if I was going to work, but he didn't like the idea and kept spitting up the milk from the bottle and screaming. Finally, Mama said I'd have to stay living with her and John until Bertie calmed down, and I could see there wasn't no other way, so we stayed on for the first month after I went back to work.

It was a nice job, not too tiring and with real pleasant people, but it was way over to the other side of town and I had to ride the bus for over an hour each way. I got up every morning at five so's I could get ready and give the children their breakfast before I left, took a six-thirty bus and rode until about twenty of eight, and then walked six blocks to my job. I got to leave at six, because although I cooked dinner I didn't have to stay to serve it, and I left soon as it was ready, rode home, and got there a little before eight. Of course, as long as we was living with Mama it was easy, 'cause I didn't have to worry none about the kids, and she wouldn't take no money from me for watching them, so I bought groceries instead.

I suppose I might not have had the push to move out after being there so long and being so comfortable, but things changed suddenly and it turned out I wasn't moving . . . they was. The man John worked for decided to move to New York and wanted John to come along, wanted him bad enough to pay for Mama and give him a raise besides, so of course they decided to go. John said I should stay in the flat and try to find someone to share it with me who could help with the kids, and that sounded like a good idea, and he even paid half the next month's rent to help me out until I could make some arrangements. I told Mrs. Gold, the lady I was working for, about needing somebody to watch the kids, and she said if I didn't have nobody to leave them with after Mama left I could bring them along until I found somebody, so that's what I started doing. They loved it, and I liked having them near, but it made it awful hard. I had to have them washed, dressed, fed, and ready to go along with me when I left at six thirty, and that took a heap of doing, especially since all of them was under six years old and not much good at doing for themselves. They really was good kids, though, and Jackie, being the oldest, did help as much as she was able, and somehow we managed.

The bus driver got used to seeing us all waiting when he drove up, and he even helped me on, seeing as how I was carrying Bertie and had Anthony and James kind of attached to my skirt. After a few days of this, a man who always seemed to be on that bus started getting down and helping so's the driver didn't have to, and pretty soon we started talking to each other and got friendly. He was about ten years older than me, I figured, which would put him in his early thirties, and he had a nice face and a real soft voice, and he was very sweet with the kids and real gentlemanly with me. He told me he worked for the Civil Service and had been to college and traveled some, and I could tell from the way he talked that he was educated. He sounded like Alice, but instead of using all the words he knew to slice you up, he used them to make you feel good, and it sure was nicer that way.

At first he was just on the bus in the morning, but after a while he managed to be on it coming home, too, and did I ever find that a comfort. The kids were always tired and cranky by that time, and having him along really helped, particularly since he liked to tell them stories. He was the greatest storyteller I ever met, and there didn't seem to be any end to the things he knew, and I enjoyed listening to him just as much as the kids did, I think. Pretty soon he asked if he could come and see us at home on a Sunday, and I was real pleased, 'cause I really liked him. He took to going to the public library and getting out children's books and reading them out loud when he came over, and I started asking him to stay to dinner, and in a little while it was like we had always known him. His name was Cornelius, and of course the kids couldn't say that, so we all called him Corny; but he said he thought Connie would be better, and that's what it became.

One Sunday he showed up with books for the kids and one for me. He said he brought it because it was a favorite of his and he thought I might like it, and if I wanted to, after the kids went to bed we could read it out loud together. It was called *Native Son* and it was the story of a black man, written by a black man, and I suppose, in a way, Connie and that book changed my life. I hadn't given much thought, up to then, about black people in general or about how tough things always seemed to be for them, 'cause with me it was always me I was living with and worrying about, and it didn't really seem to make much difference that other people had troubles, too. I knew, in a kind of dim way, about slaves and Lincoln and the War between the States, and Booker T. Washington and people like that, but they were history, and I was now.

Native Son was like the key that opened up my mind to the world, and Connie, who was never happier than when he was teaching somebody something, was so excited 'cause I took to reading and talking about what we read that he started bringing me four or five books at a time, books on every kind of subject, not just on black people. He brought me a book called *The Grapes of Wrath* and told me it was based on some things that really happened, and I was surprised to find out that white people went hungry and sometimes didn't have a place to sleep and were treated bad by the folks they worked for.

At first I don't think I even really believed it, but after Connie started bringing other books about the great things and the rotten things in our country, it began to seem real, and I noticed when I was out on the street I started really looking at the white people like they was people, instead of just white. He brought books in rhyme sometimes, and when I didn't understand some of the poems, he'd sit for hours telling me about the life of the poet who wrote that particular poem and what he was trying to say, and I noticed that when Connie was reading or talking about what we was reading it was like he came alive. He was always gentle and kind and a little washed out, but when he got going on those books or on the past, even his voice got deeper, and his eyes would flash, and he even looked bigger. At first I just noticed but didn't say nothing, but one night when we had just finished reading a book by a young Jewish girl who was killed by the Nazis and Connie was carrying on about the bravery of the human spirit, I couldn't help saying what I was thinking.

"You look like you about to lead a revolt or build a new country, or somethin' like that. I'd be downright scared if I was to meet you in a dark alley."

He kind of grinned like he was embarrassed, and I guess maybe he was.

"I do get kind of carried away, don't I? I can't help it, though, it's all so real and so touching, the things that people endure and survive and eventually beat. You can't help but admire them, can you?"

I hadn't thought about it much.

"I don't know," I said slowly. "Seems like you do what you have to do and endure what you have to endure. Ain't so much bravery as necessity."

He laughed. "If you wanted to sum up the essential difference between the thinker and the doer, you couldn't have done a better job than that sentence. But can't you hear the bravery in what you just said? The acceptance of pain and the willingness to face it and conquer it—that's bravery of the highest kind."

I guess the surprise I felt must have showed on my face, because he began to laugh until the tears ran down his face, at my expression and what I said.

"You mean there's a choice?"

When he stopped laughing he got up from his chair and came over to the couch where I was. He sat down and took my hand and he said, like he couldn't really believe it, "You never thought about there being any other way, did you? According to you, if you're in pain, or in danger, there's no choice but to fight back, right? You don't think about the odds, or that it might be hopeless—you just fight back the best way you can . . . and you don't think there's any bravery involved in that. Ossie, you're unbelievable."

I thought about what he said, and I remembered plenty of times when things seemed too tough for me to bear and I remembered, too, how I wouldn't let myself think that way.

"You can't think about how it might be hopeless, 'cause that way you make it hopeless even if it ain't. You want the strength to fight, you gotta think you can win. Can't nobody win without thinking there's at least a chance."

All of a sudden he looked kinda sick, and he stood up and went and stood at the window with his back to me.

"God, you're so young." His voice sounded kind of like he was in pain.

"What's that got to do with it?"

"After you've lived a while longer and you've fought more battles where the cards were stacked against you right from the start and you never had a chance, you'll find out what I mean, but for now, you just go on the way you are . . . and Lord knows, I wish you luck."

I shook my head. "I don't think it's like that at all. My granddaddy told me nobody can hurt you as bad as you can hurt yourself, and it sounds to me like you ain't never learned that, so maybe in return for you teaching me about books and the like, I can teach you something."

He turned to face me, with a look of such tenderness on his face that for no reason that I could see, I wanted to cry.

"You really mean that, don't you?"

I didn't rightly know what he was driving at, and it seemed like a foolish question.

"Sure I do. I wouldn't say it less'n I meant it."

"Of course you wouldn't. Everything about you is so real, so honest, so dependable. I think that's what I sensed in you from the first minute I saw you climbing onto that bus, covered with children."

He came back and sat down next to me and gently took me in his arms, soothing my hair back from my face and looking in my eyes like he was trying to see down inside of me.

"I love you, Ossie," he said. "I love you and I want to live with you, to sleep with you and eat with you and read with you and never have to leave. Would you like that?"

"You mean you want to move in, to live here with me and the kids?"

He nodded. "You said you needed somebody to help out with the rent didn't you?"

I laughed. "I wasn't thinking of no gentleman roommate, you know. I ain't never had one of those."

"Then it's high time you did. I don't wear hair pins to leave in the bathroom or nylons that I hang over the towel bar and that drip on the floor, and I've got a good steady job, and I'm not particular about what I eat, and at night when the lights are out I make a big heating pad for your cold feet. What girl can beat that offer?"

"Not any that I ever heard tell of. Only thing is, another girl wouldn't say she loved me and then expect me to say it back to her." I was very serious now.

"I don't remember even asking you to say it. It's enough for me that *I* love *you*. All I'm asking is that you let me share your life, even for a little while. Any time you want me to leave, I promise I'll go without causing you any trouble."

And that's the way Connie came to live with us. It worked out fine right from the start, because with him paying half the rent and giving me money for his food, I had enough from what I was making to pay a girl to come in and watch the kids, and that pleased me. It always seemed better to me when they could stay home than when I had to drag them to somebody else's house, and this way they was the only kids she was watching and so they got better care. Connie and I still rode the bus together every day, but now that he knew he was going to see me in the evening he didn't hang around downtown so's he could ride home with me and instead came home early and gave the kids their dinner. It was just like being married, except we wasn't.

At the beginning I never thought about it. I had been married once, and that was enough, and the way things were between Connie and me was just fine. We was together because we wanted to be, and we wouldn't be tied together if we wanted out.

If I could have made up the kind of man I wanted to marry, Connie would have been that man. He was kind, soft-spoken, gentle, honest, a tender and exciting lover, and he was good to my kids, but with all that he acted sort of like I was doing him a favor to talk to him, and it was that part that kept me from loving him, I think. He knew so much and he never was uppity or made fun of me, just used what he knew to teach me, and he never stopped trying to get me to finish school.

"If you want to go to night school," he kept saying, "I'll stay with the kids."

"What do I need school for when I've got you? I learn more from listening to you and reading the books you pick out for me than I ever could learn in a school, and I like it better this way, too.

He shook his head, dead serious.

"I can't give you a diploma, no matter how much you learn from me, and a diploma's something you and everybody else should have."

I laughed. "I don't need no diploma to wash somebody's dirty dishes. The kind of work I do, they don't want to know how many words you got in your head, just how many muscles you got in your arms. No, I don't need no diploma, but I do need to learn what you're teaching me. Besides, look at you. You not only got a high school diploma, you even been to college, and you ain't nothing but a clerk down to the county office."

"That's because I'm the wrong color." He sounded bitter, for the first time since I knew him. "And because I was born too soon. One of these days the only thing that's going to matter is how much do you know, not what color you are. You're younger than I am; it might even happen while you're young enough to have it make a difference."

"I know some black men who are lawyers and doctors and engineers and such, and they ain't as smart as you, nowhere near as smart. Seems like you could be more than a clerk, even being the color you are."

He looked angry. "*Black* lawyers and *black* doctors, living in the ghetto, treating *black* patients, defending *black* clients. It's the same as being in jail. At least I work around other kinds of people, I mix some with the white world, I get a chance to hear another point of view, to know how the white man thinks."

"You don't need that to know how the white man thinks," I laughed. "He thinks you ain't as good as he is, and as long as you know he thinks that, I can't imagine what else you need to know about him."

"It's that kind of thinking that's kept the black man a slave, that insane refusal to look at reality. This is a *white* country, and we're a minority in it, and the only way we're going to ever be equal is to learn to outwhite the white man, get so much better at the things he's good at that he's going to *have* to include us, because he'll need us. How do you think the Jews have survived all this time? Not by being willing to be stupid slobs, that's for sure."

What he said made a lot of sense, but it didn't add up to what he did, and it sure puzzled me.

"How come it don't work for you, then? You got brains and book-learning and you look around you and know what you see . . . so how come it ain't helped you more?"

He stopped looking all fired up and just looked kinda sick.

"Don't use me as an example. It's like a war, this being black in a white country, and in a war some of the soldiers are brave and some aren't, and the ones that aren't, you just can't do anything about. Even though I can't do it, I *know* education is the ammunition the black soldiers have to have."

I didn't argue no more, but I couldn't help thinking to myself that all the schooling in the world wasn't going to help as long as it didn't go along with some gumption. Connie always tried to make me think he was different than most other men, but I didn't see where, except he talked better, and talking ain't doing.

I suppose I might have gone to school like he wanted me to, except I got pregnant again. I didn't tell Connie right away, because I didn't really want to have another baby, and I wanted time to think it over. I figured that as soon as I told him he was going to get all excited and start wanting to get married, and although I didn't rightly know why, I had an uneasy feeling about the whole thing, like no matter what I did it wasn't going to come out right. I figured he'd want to get married and I wouldn't, and I was wrong on both counts. It must have been that all that learning had dulled my feelings and I couldn't figure things out very clear. When you don't know anything but what you figure out by yourself, and then you start finding out that there are other ways of looking at things, it takes a while to make everything come together, and I hadn't learned yet how to do it. Now I know how to listen to myself and believe what I hear, but I've been through a lot since then, and that's helped considerable. It was time for another lesson.

· 18 ·

I WAS IN THE BEGINNING OF MY FIFTH MONTH AND STARTING
to look pretty round before I decided there wasn't nothing else
to do but tell Connie he was going to be a daddy. By that time
I had talked myself into the idea of marrying him, and I had
talked so good I was even beginning to warm up to the whole
thing and I was kind of looking forward to the loving evening
we would have after I broke the big news to him. I waited
until after the kids was in bed and the dishes was done and
everything was quiet for the night. He was sitting on the
couch with that look of being half asleep that men get when
they're well fed and comfortable, and I went and kind of
curled up next to him and put my head on his shoulder, and
he lifted his arm and put it around me. It felt good, and for a
minute nobody said anything and I could feel myself getting
drowsy, so I sat up. He looked at me with surprise.

"What's the matter? Forget something?"

I shook my head.

"I was going to sleep, and I didn't want to. Connie, I got
something to tell you."

Right away he looked interested. One of the nicest things

about Connie was that he always listened to you like he really cared what you were going to say, and that's what he was doing now. Like I usually do, I figured there was no sense in beating around the bush.

"I'm going to have a baby."

I was looking right at him, and the change that came over his face was so extreme that I couldn't believe my own eyes. He went from looking warm and comfortable and loving to looking like he was dying, faster than I could snap my fingers. His skin got to be a kind of gray color, and the expression on his face made me think of the way Erna looked when she was took with the heart attack—stricken and kind of surprised. He didn't say a word, just sat there looking sick. It sure as hell wasn't what I expected, and I was kind of put out, so I didn't say anything, just waited for him.

"Are you sure?" His voice was as gray as his face.

"I'm sure." Disappointment made me sound even more short than I meant to, and I could see him kind of shrivel.

"Is it too late to . . . I mean, could you do anything about it?"

The contempt I felt made me forget that I had spent some time thinking about the same thing before I made up my mind I could never do that, and all I remembered was that he was willing to share my house and my bed, but not my problems . . . and that made him just like all the others I had known. I gave him a look that I hoped showed exactly how I felt, and I guess it did, 'cause he got to his feet and started to pace up and down while he tried to explain how *he* felt.

"It kills me when you look at me like that, and I don't blame you." His words said one thing, but his tone said something else, and it made me squirm, 'cause it was so mealy-mouthed. "I should have figured this might happen, but you always seemed so strong and sure of everything, and I thought you were taking care of the precautions."

"I don't know what made you think that. We never even mentioned it that I can remember. Besides, what's so all-fired awful about having a baby? I done it before, and there ain't much to it."

"Shut up! That's nigger talk!"

I was so surprised I probably sat there with my mouth open. Connie—who never got mad, who never hollered, who always made me feel like everything I did or said was all right with him—was looking at me like he wanted to kill me.

"What you talking about? I only said the truth. Ain't much to having a baby, that's all I said."

"That's right!" he yelled. "Ain't much to having a baby, not when you have it like a dog has a litter, like a cow has a calf . . . without thought, without responsibility, without caring what happens to the poor misbegotten thing once it's born. Any bitch can give birth, any stupid black girl can open her legs and let a prick in and then nine months later let a baby out. There's no trick to that, is there?"

I was really mad now. He was talking like I was some kind of dirt and like he hadn't had nothing to do with the whole thing. Like always, when I get mad I kind of tighten up inside, and what comes out of my mouth sounds much tougher than I feel.

"You feel that way about it, you can pack up and git. I managed before, and I'll do it again."

He stopped his pacing and stood and just looked at me, and then he sat down on the couch and put his head in his hands and started to cry. For a minute I felt so sorry for him I wanted to take him in my arms and try to make him feel better, but then the truth hit me, and looking at him I could see Charles, who ran out on the army and on me 'cause he wasn't no man; and Augie, who did what his mama said 'cause he wasn't no man; and Jim, who wouldn't be guardian for me and my kids 'cause he wasn't no man; and Nero, who tried to get even with the world by hurting himself and the people he loved 'cause he wasn't no man . . . and all the hurt and the hate that I had inside me came and sat on my tongue and like to gag me, and I had to get it out or choke.

"You got a right to cry. If I was you, I'd cry, too, knowing so much and none of it making me able to be a man. You got your fancy words and your books and your big brain, but you ain't got no balls, so what good is the rest? Sure, like you

said, it's easy for a girl to open her legs and let a prick in and
a baby out, but it's even easier for the boy that's attached to
that prick, ain't it? He don't have to wait around no nine
months, and he don't have to care that he's fathered a baby
. . . oh, no, he just have to have a good time and run. You
make me sick, all of you! You so all-fired sorry for yourselves
'cause you black and you mad at the world, and instead of
taking it out on the people who hurting you, you take it out
on your women and children, 'cause that's safe. You all
cowards, all mouth and no guts!" I was practically screaming,
and shaking all over, and panting like I'd run a mile.

"And don't you look down your nose at us niggers! What
you think you are? There ain't nothing wrong with being
what you mean by nigger, neither. You take a look around at
the black women you talking about like they was pigs, and you
gonna see a bunch of people being more responsible than they
rightly got the strength to be, 'cause after we open our legs
and let the black babies out, there ain't no black daddy around
to help. Hell no, while we're working and sweating and taking
care of our kids, their daddies are drinking and running and
screwing and telling themselves that they licked before they
start, so they might as well not start . . . and they leaving
us holding the bag. I may not know what's in them books you
so all-fired crazy about, but I know when I have a baby I
make a promise to the Lord to see that that baby's taken care
of, and if I make a promise I got to keep it!"

There wasn't a sound after I stopped talking. He just sat
there looking at me, but I could tell he wasn't seeing me, not
at all. He had lost the look he had before and he seemed to be
pulling himself together right in front of my eyes, and finally,
like he was remembering who he was, he stood up, real tall.

"You're right, of course. Only don't forget, you don't know
what it feels like, this trying to be a man in a society that
never could afford to let you be a man. When you're a little
boy, you want to grow up and do all the things men do—
work and make money, fall in love, marry, have children, and
have those children look at you with respect and admiration.
You want to be strong so your woman can lean on you when

she needs to, and you want to be strong so you can lean on her sometimes without being ashamed. You start out that way, but then you look around your house and you see that either your daddy's not there at all or if he is it's your mother who has to go out to work to help keep the food in your mouth, and you begin to doubt that you can do better than your daddy could. You see how tired your mother is when she gets home, and you try to tell her how much you love her, and how when you grow up you'll take care of her, but because you're black, and because she loves you, she has to make you face the world the way it really is so you don't get killed, and before you even really get started on your dreams, she takes them away. She teaches you that you have to be careful, she teaches you that when you go to school and hear about equality and liberty and justice it doesn't mean you, she teaches you that you better not dream about really being somebody, and if you have to dream you better not let the white man know you're dreaming, and she teaches you that the penalty for not listening can be death.

"If you really learn the lesson, you look at your father with new eyes and you understand why he drinks and why he doesn't seem to care that your mother stands on her feet all day in some white woman's kitchen and then comes home to work all evening in her own. He cares, God how he cares, but he can't do anything about it and the pain gets too much, so he blocks it out and keeps it blocked out with a bottle. And then, because he's been taught, just like you have, that if he shows his resentment to the white man he'll pay for it with his blood, he keeps it inside until he can't control it any more and then lets it out in the only safe place . . . on his own people, on his wife and his children and on himself. When a black man says 'nigger' the way I said it before, he's just expressing the disgust he feels for himself and for the coward he's had to become in order to survive. That's why the thought of being responsible for a baby is more than I can bear. Every time I look at it, I'll know I've condemned another human being to the hell of being alive, and that's the worst sin of all."

I didn't know what to say. Everything he said was true, and

somehow I had always known it without thinking about it, but I knew there was something more, some important thing that he hadn't mentioned or didn't want to think about.

"I know it ain't easy for you," I said slowly, "but it ain't easy for nobody, and even if what you say is the way it is, well, that don't change the fact that we *are* going to have a baby. It's real, and it's here inside me, and in a few months it's going to be ready to come out. You said things was going to change, maybe even soon enough for us to see it happen, so maybe it'll be an easier world for our baby—and you're so smart and you know so much that you could teach him and help him and . . ."

"Don't do that!" His voice was sharp. "Don't start planning for me and trapping me in your hopes. I'll let you down, just like I've always done to everybody who tried to make me do what I couldn't do, what I can't do."

"It ain't *can't*," I snapped. "It's *won't*. You so damned set on seeing it like it is, well then, see it all, not just what makes you feel good." Suddenly I knew what was missing from what he had said, what was missing from him and all the men like him.

"Sure it's rotten to be a black man! It ain't no picnic to be a black woman, either, believe me, but it don't have to be as rotten as you say it is. My granddaddy tried to teach me that a long time ago. He said you gotta make do with what you got. You got to do the best you can to change what needs changing, but until it gets changed you got to live so's you can respect yourself no matter how rough it is. Listening to you and the other guys I've known, I ain't never heard nothing about self-respect, 'cause you ain't got none. You all think 'cause you've gotten a lousy break that gives you the right to lay down and die, and you've convinced yourself and your women that there ain't nothing else you can do, but you don't really believe it. You know you're laying down when you should be standing up, and that's why you hate yourself so much. You're no good to you, so how can you be good to anybody else? Here you going to be a daddy, and you've read so much and you've thought so much and you say you know the answers to what's wrong . . . well, here's your chance to start teaching somebody else so that when he grows up the same things that happened to you won't happen to him. Maybe it *is* too late for you, but that don't mean it's too late for your son."

He shook his head.

"I know you can't understand," he said, very low. "Maybe you're right. Maybe we've made our women so strong by being so weak, but whatever the reason, that's the way it is. You look at things the way your granddaddy said and no doubt he was a better man than I am, but I can't be him. Not *won't, can't*. It's too late, Ossie; I can't change. Just the thought of being responsible for another human being when my hands are tied and I can't even help myself . . . it's more than I can stand."

All at once all my sympathy and all my trying to understand disappeared. I only knew that his child was coming to life inside of me and, like usual, I was on my own.

"You make me want to puke!" My rage gave me words to hurt him with. "You, standing there feeling so sorry for yourself, thinking about you, you, you . . . what about me? What about your baby? Even if you don't owe me anything, you sure as hell owe him! What about that?"

"I told you before. When it comes to emotional debts, I'm a deadbeat. I'm sorry . . . I'm truly sorry."

He went to the hall closet, got out his coat, and slowly put it on.

"Don't worry," he said. "I'll try to get some money to give you. I might be able to do that, but I can't do the rest, and you're better off knowing the truth so you can plan for the future."

I hated him. I hated him so much there didn't seem to be words enough to tell him.

"You see that you get me some money." My voice was like ice. "You ain't good for nothing else. And don't bring it . . . send it. I don't like throwing up, and if I see your face again, I might."

"Good-by, Ossie," he said. "You've got the guts to take your own advice. I hope you do."

The door closed after him, and all at once the mad went out

of me. I thought about running after him, but there had been such a sadness in his voice that I kind of knew it wouldn't change nothing no matter what I did. I was so tired, like I'd been running all day, and I knew there wasn't nothing I could do right then, so I got undressed and went to bed, but as tired as I was I couldn't sleep. I kept hearing Connie's voice and seeing his face and remembering how he looked when he read to me and was all happy and excited, and how it felt when he was in bed and he was so gentle and so warm . . . and the whole thing made me cry. Once I got started, I couldn't seem to stop, and I spent the whole night lying in my tears. Finally, by the time I had cried myself out, it was time to get up and go to work, and while I was getting dressed I tried to plan what to do next, but I couldn't get myself together enough to be sensible, so I called Mrs. Gold and told her I was sick and wouldn't be in, and went back to bed. I was so worn out I even let Margie, the girl who took care of the kids, come and take them out, and I just laid on top of my bed, not thinking, not feeling, just being. I must have finally gone to sleep, 'cause when the doorbell rang it really made me jump.

There was two policemen standing there.

"You know a man named Cornelius Boland?"

I nodded.

"He lives here with you, right?"

I nodded again.

"You related to him?"

"What's wrong?" While I was asking the question, I knew the answer.

"He's dead." The policeman who was doing the talking said the words out flat. The other one added, meaning to be kind, "He walked in front of a bus. Couldn't have suffered none; it smashed him flat as a pancake."

I didn't say anything. I couldn't.

"The body, or what's left of it, is down at the morgue. You call this number."

He held out a card to me, and I took it without really knowing what I was doing.

"You know any of his folks?"

I shook my head again.

"Well, we'll check him out. You call later, you hear?"

They turned around and walked away, leaving me standing looking after them. I felt like I couldn't move, like the horror of what they said had turned me to stone, and I felt like stone inside, too. No pain, no tears, just a feeling of weighing a thousand pounds outside and two thousand inside. Finally, I kind of dragged myself back inside to the couch and sat down, and I was still sitting, staring into space, when Margie came back with the kids. I didn't tell her what had happened, just let her leave, and I gave the kids their dinner and talked to them and undressed them and put them to bed, all the time not feeling anything but heavy. And then, when they was asleep, I made myself some coffee and sat down to think about what to do.

I tried, really tried to plan, but all I could see was Connie's face when he left, and all I could hear was his voice saying, "You've got the guts to take your own advice. I hope you do." I wasn't sure what advice he was talking about, and I tried to go back over what we had said and finally I remembered what he meant. It was about owing the new baby something, and about teaching him so's his world wouldn't be as lousy as ours . . . and, it seemed to me, it was about changing what you could change and making do with the rest. I didn't know where to begin, not yet, but I knew I couldn't ever go back to being the only one in the world. If I wanted my kids to have a chance, I had to start paying attention to what was going on around them, to other kids and how they lived, 'cause between them all they was going to make the world different —maybe better, maybe worse, but different.

· 19 ·

LIKE SOMETIMES HAPPENS WHEN YOU'VE REACHED THE END OF one road, another one opened up for me. First off, I knew I couldn't go on being so bullheaded any more. The days of me against the world was over, and I could see I needed help. I told Mrs. Gold the truth about being pregnant and about Connie being killed, and she said I could work full time or part time or any way I wanted, and I could bring the kids with me if I wanted. Then I went down to the county, 'cause I was old enough now, and I signed up for help. They didn't treat me any better or any worse than before, just looked down their noses when I said I was going to have another baby, and told me I had to go to birth-control clinic for lectures after the baby was born! I hated to lie to them about me working, but I knew from experience that what they gave me wasn't going to be enough, and I had to add to it the best way I could.

Then after I done all that, I took the kids and went back to The Other Side of the Hill to see Lila and find out what happened to Nero—and I was sure glad I did, 'cause when I got there she was real happy to see me and told me that Nero had gone away and said he wasn't coming back no more. She said she missed him, but she was glad he went 'cause he scared her when he had what she called his "spells," and she was getting too old to be scared like that. After I told her what had happened to me, she invited me to move back in, and I was real glad to 'cause that way she could lie to the social worker for me if I wasn't there when she came, and I knew she'd watch out for the kids when I went to have the baby.

After a few weeks of living back on The Other Side of the Hill it was like we'd never been away. The kids was real happy to be back with Lila's kids, and I didn't have to take them to work with me, which was a big help, and I was trying to lay a little by to tide me over after the baby was born. Mrs. Gold kept worrying about me working so hard when I was getting near my time, and it got almost funny after a while, 'cause lots of times when I got to her house she had all the real heavy work done already and what was left for me was a breeze. She was a real nice woman, a kind woman, but sometimes the way she looked at me I could tell she thought I was shiftless, having so many kids with no man to help out. Maybe if I'd tried to explain she would have understood, but I still hadn't learned that most people want to help if you give them a chance to really know what you're like, and I just let her go on thinking what she wanted. We spent a lot of time in the same house, but I didn't really understand about her, and she didn't really understand about me . . . and that's what has to be different some day, if we gonna be able to live together, like most decent folks hope we can.

Being back on aid, it wasn't no problem for me to go back to the county hospital to have the baby, and after having so many it was real easy. I wasn't in labor more than about an hour when Linda was born, and two hours after that I felt good enough to get up, but of course I didn't. Back then they figured most mothers only got any rest when they was in the hospital, so they kept you for five days, and as long as I knew Lila was looking after the other kids I kind of enjoyed myself. In the ward we all kind of helped each other out, and a baby ward is usually a happy place, so it was nice and friendly. There was two girls who were having their first babies, and they was very young and kind of scared, so I told them about my kids and made the whole thing sound easier than it was, and they perked up some. I figured the less scared they was about how to help a child come up, the better it would be for both of them, and it sure couldn't hurt none.

Linda was the spitting image of Connie, with a straight, narrow nose and big brown eyes, and when they brought her in to nurse she looked up at me like Connie come back to life, and it gave me a turn every time it happened. Watching her at my breast, I prayed she'd have Connie's brain and the guts to use it, knowing that with a combination like that she'd be ahead of the game right from the start.

Mrs. Gold sent me a plant to the hospital, with a note saying she was closing up her apartment for a few months while she and her husband went on a trip, so while it was nice of her to send the plant, I was kind of depressed at losing the work. I could have sat there and worried, and I started to, but then I reminded myself that I'd managed up to now one way or another, and I'd probably go right on managing, so I put the whole thing out of my mind and enjoyed the rest.

The day before I was supposed to go home, they come and wheeled me down to the birth-control clinic, like they had said they was going to. There was about thirty women there, more black ones than white ones, but enough of both so's you'd know it wasn't just the black who was ignorant. They had a lady lecturing on birth-control methods, and she had graphs and slides and knew what she was talking about, but it struck me that the mistake the birth-control people made was in lecturing instead of talking to the other women and letting them talk back. Judging by myself, I knew that the reason I kept having babies wasn't because I didn't know how to prevent them, it was because I didn't believe in not having them, and I'll bet a lot of those women sitting there felt pretty much like I did, and of course if you feel like that you just let the lecture slide over you, and it don't mean much of anything. Later, when I started working with kids and I saw how wrong I had always been about having babies, I had some groups of girls, and we got together and talked about having babies, and mostly I listened and they talked, and there was quite a few who thought the Lord intended them to have as many babies as possible—just like I used to think. Some of the other girls pointed out that if that was the case the Lord would have provided food and clothes and better houses for all those babies, and although I knew there was a lot more to it than that, I figured we'd made a gain right there.

When I took Linda home, Lila and all the kids was real glad to see both of us, and Jackie started right in treating Linda like she was a doll. The younger kids didn't pay her much mind after the first few minutes, but Jackie really cottoned up to her, and it's been that way ever since. It's like Linda's had two mothers, me and Jackie, and as far as I can see it didn't do no harm.

The first night I was home, after all the kids was tucked away, Lila poured us out some coffee, and we sat down to talk. I told her about Mrs. Gold and how I didn't have no job, but she said not to worry 'cause she thought she knew where I could get one as soon as I was strong enough to be on my feet for eight hours.

"You going to be a cocktail waitress," she said proudly. "No more kitchens and scrubbing other people's floors. From now on you wear a real perky outfit and serve drinks to thirsty gentlemen. Even if your lady wasn't going away, with a chance at a job like this I figured you'd take it, so I told them you'd be ready to go to work about a week from now. That all right with you?"

"How much it pay?" It didn't matter much to me what kind of work I did, long as I could do it, but more than anything I wanted to earn enough so's I could take care of the kids without no help. It wasn't that I was ashamed to be on aid, 'cause I knew it wasn't through no fault of mine I needed the money, but I hated having to answer to anybody for what I did, and I knew as long as the county was dishing out dollars they was going to have the right to ask me questions and look down their nose at me, and I didn't like it. When Lila told me what the pay was, I decided right then and there that I was born to be a cocktail waitress, 'cause even though it wasn't a lot, what with tips and all, I figured I could manage alone, and besides, working in the evening meant I could be home with the kids in the daytime, and that would have almost made up my mind anyhow.

"Why should I wait a whole week to start?" I demanded. "I'm feeling fine right this minute. You just tell me who to see and I'll go over there first thing tomorrow and tell him I'm ready now."

She shook her head. "You *think* you're ready now, but you ain't. You start standing on your feet all night right after you have a baby and you end up flat on your face. What you in such a all-fired rush for, anyhow? You got a roof over your head and you and the kids ain't about to die from hunger neither, so next week'll be as good as this week."

"I wouldn't rest, anyhow, worrying that the job would be gone when I was ready," I answered. "Just you tell me who to see and don't worry about me, okay? I know how I feel better than you do, right?"

"You as stubborn as a mule, and you ain't going to listen to me, and you'll be sorry," she said darkly. "I'm older than you and I was just as bull-headed when I was young, and now I can't hardly stand on my feet. My mama tried to tell me . . ."

"And you didn't listen, right?" I interrupted. "If you was so much like me, then you should understand I ain't going to listen, either. Who do I see?"

Lila sighed. "Okay, it's your funeral. His name is Bill Bronson, and it's Bronson's Bar and Grill, over to Center Street. Just tell him who you are, 'cause he's expecting you, but not so soon."

I patted her shoulder.

"Thanks, Lila. If I fall on my face like you say, you can have the good feeling that comes from saying I told you so."

"You shut up!" Her tone was mad, but her face wasn't. "One thing I can't stand, it's a smart nigger."

"Then I don't have to worry," I said. "I'm about the dumbest one around."

The next morning I put on my sharpest-looking outfit and

went to the Bronson Bar and Grill . . . and it was closed. I
just hadn't stopped to think about what time the place opened
'cause I was so anxious to nail down the job, and when I got
there it was shut up tighter than a drum, with a sign on the
front saying it opened at eleven o'clock. I didn't have no
watch, but I figured I was about two hours too early, and I
wasn't about to go back home. There was a bench where the
bus stopped, so I figured I'd sit down in the sun and wait. It
was real pleasant sitting there with the warm sun on my back,
and I guess I wasn't as strong as I thought, 'cause it felt mighty
good to sit down and it seemed like one minute I was enjoying the sun and the next a man was poking me gently in the
shoulder and saying, "You slept through five buses. Ain't you
going nowhere?"

"What time is it?" For all I knew I had been sleeping all day.

"A quarter to eleven. You late for something?"

"I hope not." Nervously, I was patting my hair and trying
to get myself back together. "I guess they don't hire cocktail
waitresses early in the morning, do they?"

He smiled. "I can't rightly remember any cocktail waitresses
asking to be hired or fired or anything else before about three
o'clock. If they good waitresses, though, I don't think it matter
much what time they come asking. You trying to get a job at
Bronson's?"

I nodded. "I think I already got it, 'cause my friend talked
to Bronson about me, and she says it's all set. It's just that I
wanted to know if I could start sooner than she said.

"I sure as hell hope he says okay." The man smiled.

"What difference it make to you? You a customer there?"

"Nope, I work there. Part-time bartender and general
handyman and sometimes bouncer. That's when I ain't working at my other job, of course."

"No wonder jobs is hard to get. You got them all tied up."

He laughed, and I noticed what a nice friendly face he had.

"It sounds like it, sure enough. I'm really a construction
worker by trade, but being black, you put in a lot of lay-off
time, so when I ain't building I work in the bar. I kind of like

it, 'cause that way I get a change. C'mon, I'll walk in with you. I'll even introduce you to the boss if you tell me your name. Mine's Guffy."

"Mine's White."

"You only got one name?"

"No, I got two, but you only told me one of yours, so I figured one of mine was enough."

He smiled."Clarence Guffy . . . now you know why I only told you one. Don't nobody call me nothing but Guffy, any-how. What your friends call you . . . White?"

"Not so's you'd notice. Mostly they call me Ossie."

He reached down and took my hand. "Okay, Ossie, let's go get you a job."

Mr. Bronson turned out to be a real nice man who was happy about my starting right away. At first I couldn't figure out whether he was black or white, 'cause it was pretty dark in the bar and he sure didn't seem to be the same color as Guffy or me, so when he walked away for a minute to answer the phone, I asked Guffy.

"Don't nobody rightly know the answer to that one," Guffy admitted. "He looks white and acts and talks black, and as far as I know, ain't nobody ever asked him, and he ain't never said. We kind of figured he's mostly white, but not all, and being mostly white around here means you're black, so we just let it go at that. Ain't nothing to worry about, nohow."

"I ain't worried about that."

"Maybe not, but you didn't look too comfortable when you was talking to him, I noticed."

"That's because I never done this kind of work before, and I didn't know if I should tell him, that's all."

Guffy looked amused. "You ever lived with a man?"

My back went up. "What kind of a question it that?"

"A straight-out question. If you ever lived with a man, well then, you waited on him some, and if you know how to do that, you know how to be a cocktail waitress. You just keep the customer happy, get him his drinks, keep the ash trays cleaned, and learn how to duck with a smile when he makes a grab for you. Think you can do that?"

Just then Mr. Bronson came back, and he told me pretty much the same thing. He showed me the uniform I had to wear and said if it fit me I wouldn't have to pay for nothing but to keep it clean, and as far as he could see, wasn't no reason why I couldn't start the next afternoon, and that's what I did. The first couple of days I was pretty jumpy, being afraid all the time that I was doing something wrong, but pretty soon I could see that whatever being a cocktail waitress needed, I had, and then I relaxed and kind of enjoyed it. It wasn't all that great, but it was sure better than housework, and what with the guarantee Mr. Bronson paid and the tips left by the customers, I was able to manage fine and not need help from the county any more. Of course, if it hadn't been for Lila, it wouldn't have worked out that way, but she was there and I was grateful. There ain't nothing that feels as good as knowing you can provide for yourself and your kids, and it's the kind of feeling that really keeps you from bein' scared.

During the week there was only me, Guffy, and Mr. Bronson working, but on Friday and Saturday nights, which was when the big rush come, there was Boyd, who worked the bar, and Callie, a cocktail waitress on weekends and a student the rest of the time. She was kind of over-age for a college girl, being about thirty, and she talked a lot like Connie had, and when she found out I had read some and liked to talk about books she looked so surprised that I got mad.

"Ain't no call for you to be so shook up," I told her, with considerable frost. "Just because I ain't been to college don't mean I don't know nothing or don't want to learn more."

"Honey, I'm sorry." She sounded like she really meant it. "I didn't mean it to look like that. It's just that I'm not used to hearing anything like that from the folks I meet. Mostly they couldn't care less about what's between the covers of books, and you can't blame them. Nobody ever let them know how much power there is in learning, or how much pleasure, either. How'd you find out about it?"

I told her a little about Connie, just enough to describe what kind of man he was.

"You still seeing him?"

I shook my head. "He's passed on," I said shortly.

"Gee, honey, I'm sorry." She put her hand on my arm. "Isn't it ironic the way the good ones die and the bastards live on?"

I nodded, even though I wasn't too sure what ironic meant. The meaning of what she was saying was clear enough so's not knowing the word didn't confuse it none, but I went and looked it up anyhow, and after I got used to it, I found myself thinking that the real irony of Connie was that he was a good man and a bastard all at the same time. I was still pretty young when I was thinking that, 'cause now I know that combination of good and evil shows up in mostly everybody, one way or another. Like with Callie. She went out of her way to get me a card so's I could borrow books at the Settlement House Center, and she asked me every week to go to meetings there with her, and we got to be real good friends, but her bad side had to do with money. On weekends when she was there we was supposed to split the tips, and I know for sure she lied about how much she got and pocketed some that was mine, but other than that she was so nice I didn't know what to do about it. Finally I decided to talk it over with Guffy. When I told him about it, he looked at me with surprise.

"What do you mean, you don't know what to do? Somebody was cheating me, I'd just tell 'em to stop."

"I can't do that. Supposing I was wrong?"

He gave me a hard look. "You mean you ain't sure she's doing what you say she's doing?"

Miserably, I nodded. "I'm sure all right."

"Well, make up your mind." He looked annoyed. "First you say she's cheating, then you say what if she ain't, and now you say you're sure she is. You just scared to face her with it, ain't you?"

"I guess so."

"Well, there ain't but two ways for a body to go when he wants to have a showdown with somebody but ain't got the guts. Decide if what that person is doing to him is worth fighting about or not, and then act proper to what he decides.

Which is more important to you—Callie liking you or Callie cheating you?"

While I was trying to decide, he said, like it was unimportant, " 'Course, if you don't face her with it, it ain't going to matter whether she likes you 'cause you ain't going to be able to stand the sight of her."

As soon as he said it, I knew he was right, for that time and for all time. That was the first of a long list of things that Guffy taught and is teaching me to this day, things that seem so simple when he says them that you wonder why you didn't think of it yourself, but somehow you never do. The next time Callie come to work, when we was getting dressed in the back, I told her that when I looked at the cash-register receipts on the days we both worked, it didn't look like the tip-splitting was coming out right. She didn't say nothing, but that night when we divided up I got everything that was coming to me, and from then on . . . and in a little while I forgot that it had ever happened and was able to enjoy her as my friend and sometimes teacher, and she taught me a lot.

She started out by getting me to go down to the Settlement House Center with her, like I said. She went every Wednesday afternoon 'cause that was when she taught a class in reading for kids who had problems with understanding things they saw in print. The first couple of times I just went along and sat in the back of the room and listened. They gave me a book of my own so's I could follow what was going on, and it was all pretty interesting 'cause Callie and the ten kids in the class really went at it hot and heavy when they was talking about the meaning of what they was reading. I had trouble keeping my mouth shut, 'cause I had some ideas of my own that I would like to have said, but I remembered I was just a visitor and didn't say nothing.

One Wednesday after I'd been going there for a couple of months, it was time for the class, and I was there and the kids was there, but Callie wasn't. I was just about to tell them all to go home, when one of the girls said, "Ossie, long as we're all here, why couldn't we have the class and you be the teacher?"

" 'Cause I don't know enough, that's why." The whole idea made me feel weak.

"You don't have to know much," one of the other girls said. "We could just talk about what we read, like we usually do, and you could kind of lead off, that's all."

"No," I said firmly. "Wouldn't be right and I can't do it anyhow."

All of a sudden, in my head, I heard myself saying to Connie *can't* or *won't*, and what I was thinking must have showed in my face 'cause one kid brought me a chair and the rest of them sat down in a circle around me, and before I knew what hit me, we was all talking a mile a minute. Of course we didn't wind up talking about what was in the book, but I didn't feel too bad 'cause we talked about reading and why we liked it and why we didn't, and I don't know if anybody learned anything, but it was sure interesting. One thing I *did* notice was that Roger, a boy who never said anything much, really got wound up about what was wrong with the books we was reading and like to talk so much nobody else got their fair share, but I figured that was all to the good and didn't try to stop him. I guess some of the kids must have told Callie about it, and she talked to Mr. Grant, the social worker who ran the center, and before I knew it I had a group that met after Callie's class was through—what Callie and Mr. Grant called a discussion group. I never did find out if there was anything special we was supposed to talk about, 'cause there seemed to be so many subjects that just naturally came up, and we went wherever the talk seemed to lead us.

It's been more than fifteen years now since I started doing that, and I've done it in Cincinnati and in Los Angeles with Lord knows how many kids, and when they talk about a generation gap and about how the kids who are coming up now are different than any kids who come up before, I know they're only listening to what those kids are saying on the surface. Underneath they're asking for and complaining about the same things they always did—a break, somebody to really listen when they talk, and, most of all, somebody to say when to stop—not as a threat, but as a protection.

Meeting Guffy and Callie brought me to a new place, and it's a place I seem to have been getting ready for in all the years that went before. Guffy started taking me out pretty regular, coming to the house and getting to know my kids and letting them know him, and in a few months it was like he had always been there. I could feel the love and respect I felt for him getting bigger by the day, and he didn't miss no chance to let me know how he felt about me and the kids, so it just seemed right when we started talking about getting married. At first I tried to make him see that taking me on was a pretty big deal, considering it meant taking on five kids too, but he said if I had managed to stay alive with the kids and no man to help, then it wasn't going to be that rough for him, and I'd better learn to stop worrying and let him be the one to do it. I think he knew that it would be a while before I could do that, because I was so used to being left high and dry that I was all suspicion, but like all the other things that was different about him, he didn't expect me to change all at once, but just to know what had to be different and try to make it happen.

Knowing how much easier it was to try when you didn't have to succeed in a leap helped me with my own kids and later with the kids in my groups, and I think it's the most important single thing most people overlook. Everybody says, you wrong, you know you wrong, so straighten up and fly right . . . NOW! . . . as though you could just throw a switch and become somebody else, and then when you can't do it right away you get discouraged and finally give up trying at all. The way Guffy looked at it, most people want to help themselves, and maybe if they're lucky somebody comes along and helps them see what they have to try to do, and then if they don't expect it all to happen at once, they change a little bit at a time, getting better, getting worse, but always getting a little closer to the goal. I know it worked for me, and I've seen it work with my kids and the kids in my groups, and I believe in it.

We found a little house right near Lila's, and we got married, and the seven of us moved in. I kept my job 'cause I knew Guffy couldn't start right in taking care of all of us, leastwise not until his construction work was steadier, and besides, I liked being out and meeting people. When the word got around in the bar that I had married the bouncer I didn't have to worry any more about being pawed by some drunk, and that made it easier, too. Like usual, I got pregnant right away, and a bar wasn't like some lady's kitchen; you couldn't be a cocktail waitress after you started to show too much, so I worked about seven months after we got married, and then I had to quit, and that was pretty good, 'cause by then Guffy was doing more construction work than he had before and I had put a little aside to help him out. It sure was a good feeling, knowing that there was two of us to look out for the kids and each other, and, a little at a time, I started learning to depend on somebody else.

· 20 ·

GUFFY AND I GOT MARRIED IN 1955, AND BY 1960 WE HAD FOUR
more kids—Ann, Roberto, Bryan, and Price—which, added to
the way the family started out, made eleven of us living in the
house. Of course, by then Jackie was thirteen and a real help,
and the other kids all kind of copied her and took care of each
other. Having Lila so close by, I worked whenever I could and
brought in a little extra, and Mr. Grant, knowing how many
people Guffy had to provide for, somehow found a little
money in the budget and paid me for the group work I was
doing and I was very grateful, 'cause he knew I would have
done it anyhow, but he was that kind of a man. Aside from
the money, I got more from those discussion groups than the
kids did, I think. They kept me thinking and learning, two
things lots of people don't set much store by . . . and those
are the people I'm sorry for.

Every time I had another baby, Guffy would start carrying
on about I wasn't to work no more, and who did I think I
was—a mule? And while it made me feel good that he felt
that way, I just told him I felt fine and went on doing it my
way. It wasn't strictly true that I felt fine; I was getting

tireder faster and finding it harder to get up in the morning, but with all those kids I just had to help. I don't know that I could have kept it up forever, but I didn't get a chance to find out, 'cause one day Guffy got a letter from his cousin Ben in Los Angeles, and my life changed again.

Ben was in the building-maintenanc business, and he wrote to Guffy to see if Guffy would like to come out and work for him. The letter was full of reasons why he should go, starting with the money to be made and ending with the fact that it never got cold in L.A., and that meant a real saving in winter clothes. I was ready to pack up and leave right away, but Guffy calmed me down and said it sounded good to him, but he wasn't about to move us all so far away until he went and saw for himself that Ben meant what he was saying. Besides, the money it would take to get all of us out to California would take a heap of working and saving, so he figured to go on ahead and send for us however and whenever he could.

I didn't much like the idea of his going off without me, but there wasn't no other way we could do it, and that's the way it was done. We all took Guffy to the bus station, and when he was kissing me good-by he said "see you soon," and knowing Guffy, that comforted me, 'cause he tried not to promise what he couldn't do. Ben put Guffy to work as soon as he got there, and I started getting letters raving about L.A. and how we was all going to love it, and in every letter was some money to put toward bus fare for us. I was trying to save a little, myself, but with all those kids it seemed like that was a lost cause. I knew that lots of times when families with lots of children moved far away they farmed out the kids and brought them out whenever they had the money to pay their bus fare, but I had two reasons for not wanting to do that. One was I was still hung up on keeping us together no matter what, and the other, which may have been a result of the first, was that none of the kids had ever been in any kind of trouble, and I aimed to keep it that way. The Other Side of the Hill wasn't the greatest place for kids to grow up, but if they had a home and somebody to listen and care, it looked like that was enough to keep them from getting too wild, and I just felt it wasn't right to start changing things at that point.

After Guffy sent enough for three bus fares, he suggested I come out with the two youngest children, but when I wrote and explained why I didn't want to, he agreed that maybe I was right. If he was missing me as much as I was missing him, it sure wasn't easy to wait so long till we was together again, but there didn't seem no other way. We waited, and saved a little more, but we was still a long way from having enough, and then John came back to town with Mama and solved the problem. The people he worked for had gone to California for the winter and they wanted their car out west. They had gone by plane 'cause they didn't like the long drive, but John was driving it for them, and he said the four oldest could ride with him and Mama while the others went with me on the bus, and that's the way we all got to L.A. at the same time.

Guffy's cousin Ben helped him find a place big enough for all of us, but rents were much higher in L.A. than in Cincinnati, and the place he took was in a neighborhood that wasn't even as good as The Other Side of the Hill, but we was all so glad to be together again that nobody paid no mind. The place was a house that used to be for one family, but now was for two. The owner had sliced the place down the middle by putting up walls, and those walls made some pretty crazy-shaped rooms. We turned the dining room into a bedroom and had two of the kids sleep in the living room, and that way we come out with five bedrooms, at least at night. In the morning until everything got picked up, Guffy said the place looked just like the barracks he slept in when he was in the army.

It took a while to get the kids back in school, but as soon as I did, I started looking for a part-time job like I had back home. If I could work at night while Guffy was home I wouldn't have to worry about somebody watching the kids, so I tried to go back to being a cocktail waitress, but I didn't have no luck. L.A. was so big, and we didn't have a car, and trying to get any place on the bus was having to plan to spend two or three hours traveling, not to mention the dollar or more it cost every time you rode any distance. I got pretty depressed, 'cause no matter how hard Guffy worked, he just couldn't make enough to support us all, and something had to be done. Then one night Ben come over and told me about a friend of his who had a convalescent home right near by and needed somebody for the night shift.

"What kind of job is it?" Right away, Guffy was worried I'd be working too hard.

"A kind of combination nurse and housekeeper, I guess." I could tell the way Ben said it that he didn't have no idea what his friend wanted, but even though Guffy cared, I didn't. If it gave me a chance to earn some money, then I could do it, so I figured if it was very rough, I just wouldn't tell Guffy. We needed the money real bad, and what he didn't know he didn't have to worry about.

It turned out Ben and I were both right. The owner, when I saw him next day, said the job was practical nursing, and that's what it was, except that most everybody in the home wasn't convalescing; they was just sitting there waiting to die and hoping it would be soon. There wasn't enough help, neither, so besides waiting on the patients, there was always a lot of cleaning to do, particularly since a lot of them couldn't control themselves any more and had to be cleaned up like babies. Mrs Campbell, the owner's sister, ran the place, and after I talked to her she said I'd do fine and she'd show me around if I thought I wanted the job. There was twenty rooms in the old house, and in each room was two or three poor old souls, some sick in the body, some sick in the head, and some not sick at all but just old with no family to take care of them. When I saw them, my heart got heavy and I figured anything I could do to make it a little nicer for them would be worth doing. When I get home I told Guffy the job would be real easy and set his mind at rest that way, and that's how I started living the busiest time of my life.

Every day was pretty much the same. I got up at six thirty so's I could get the five kids who went to school ready to leave by eight. We tried to all sit down to breakfast together, 'cause that was the only meal of the day we all had together, and that took a heap of doing, but Jackie and Anthony helped and so did Guffy, and we got it done. Then when we was done eating, the school kids and Guffy all left together, and me and the four little ones had the house to ourselves. After the dishes was done, there was always cleaning and picking up to do, and going to the store and such. I tried to cook stuff that the kids and Guffy could warm up, and what with the cleaning and the shopping and the cooking and all, it would suddenly be four o'clock and time to leave for work. Jackie and Anthony watched the rest of the kids until Guffy came home, and then he took it from there. Meantime, I got to the home and started eight hours of nursing, cleaning and general all-around care, and by the time I got home again, at about one in the morning, I was so tired it was an effort to take my clothes off. If it hadn't been for the weekends, I don't think I could have kept it up, but at least then I didn't have to get up so early and I rested a little. I started losing weight and looking pretty bad, and Guffy started carrying on about me quitting, but I told him I felt fine and he just worried too much. That shut him up for a couple of days, and then he started in again, but I wasn't listening.

It went on that way into spring. Looking back, I don't know how I ever did it, but I guess when you just naturally bull-headed, you don't quit until you drop, and that's just what I did. It was the Friday before Easter vacation, and I was feeling so bad that I almost didn't go to work, but then I told myself that with the vacation coming up I'd have more help in the house and I could sleep later, so I went. At about ten o'clock, Mrs. Johnson, one of the oldest of the old ladies, was took with a seizure of some kind and started throwing herself around in her bed, and we was afraid she'd get hurt, so we tried to grab her arms and legs and hold her down until the doctor came. For a weak old lady, she suddenly got terrible strong, and I was trying to keep ahold of her arms, and she was pulling and I was tugging, when a pain ripped through my middle like somebody cut me in half with a knife. I tried to keep holding her, but instead of seeing her, all I could see was black dots that got bigger and bigger until they all got together and I wasn't there no more.

When I come to, I was laying on the next bed to Mrs. Johnson, and the doctor was bending over me and saying my name. I opened my eyes, but I couldn't see him real clear, and as soon as I started even knowing where I was the pain come back and started to grow until I thought it was tearing me in two. I guess he give me a shot and in a few minutes I felt like the pain was in my body, but I was floating high above it and I didn't care. I passed out, and I mean real out, 'cause when I woke up, Guffy was sitting next to my bed, holding his head like it was going to come off if he didn't, and two nurses was working on me and I was in the hospital.

The next few weeks are just a big blur. Seems like I tore something inside of me while I was struggling with the old lady, and it would have been just a simple operation to fix it, but I was so run down they couldn't operate right away, and then when they did I didn't get over it as fast as they thought I should, and the upshot of the whole thing was I was real sick for about six weeks and then wore out for three months more. I think they would have let me go home sooner than they did, but Guffy, knowing me, told the doctor that if I come home I wouldn't stay laying down, so they kept me a long time.

Usually Guffy was right, but this time he was wrong, 'cause even when I went home and wanted to start right in taking care of things, I just didn't have the strength. And did I ever want to start taking care of things! It wasn't the kids' fault, and I knew it, but while I had been sick and Guffy was working—and when he wasn't, spending his time sitting with me in the hospital—things had gotten pretty different at home. The neighbor ladies had tried to help out, but they had their own houses and their own kids to care for, and Jackie had tried to take my place, but she was only fourteen, and things was really in a mess by the time I got home. That wouldn't have been so bad, 'cause in time I could have got it all cleaned up, but from the minute I was brought home I knew some kind of change had come over Anthony, a change that made me cold all over.

When I got sick, he was a pretty normal twelve-year-old boy, snotty sometimes, mean sometimes, real sweet when he felt like being nice, and, in general, a kid I could manage if I put my mind to it. When I come back, he was still twelve and he was still a boy, but that was all about him that was the same as when I left. First off, when he wasn't there to say hello after I got home, I thought it was funny, 'cause he was very loving with me, and I kept asking Jackie if she knew where he was, and she kept getting a funny look on her face and saying things about not worrying, he'd be back when it was time to eat, but he wasn't. Finally, about nine o'clock, I got Guffy to go out and look for him, and he was gone about an hour and finally came back with him, Guffy looking mad and Anthony looking sullen.

"Where you been?" I wasn't in no mood to treat him gentle. He didn't even look at me. "Where you been?" I repeated. "Fine thing, I come home from the hospital and you ain't even here to say hello." He got very busy, emptying out his pockets and looking at the junk he was carrying.

"I was around." He sounded like I had a hell of a nerve even asking.

"Around where?"

"Just around, that's all."

"That ain't no answer. I want to know where you been!"

"He's probably been tagging along with Bill Wilson and his gang." Jackie's voice was telling me more than her words. Her voice said Bill Wilson wasn't nobody to tag along with.

"You mind your own business!" Anthony said, real mean.

"That's enough." Guffy's voice was mad. "Where you been, you been. Now that your mother's home, you just start acting decent again, hear?"

Anthony didn't answer, but the look he give Jackie was enough to kill. I knew I wasn't going to get no place with him right then, but I decided to ask Jackie a lot of questions first chance I got. Turned out she wasn't much help. She just knew that Anthony spent most of his time out of the house

and that he spent it with a bunch of sixteen-year-old boys who
didn't really accept him but let him tag along if he did what
they told him to do. The leader of the gang, this Bill Wilson,
was a real tough who'd been off to the J.D. camp a couple of
times, and all the younger kids in the neighborhood was scared
of him and give him a wide berth if they could, but there
was something about him that turned Anthony on, or at least
so Jackie said.

As soon as I was strong enough to go out for a little while,
I started asking around the neighborhood about what was
going on, and what I heard made me sick. Seemed as though
Bill Wilson and kids like him was the new heroes around
there. Used to be that there'd always be one or two like Bill
in any neighborhood where poor kids lived, but now, suddenly, if they wasn't like Bill, they was busy trying to get to
be like him. Seemed like all the boys figured being tough was
the answer to all the things they saw around them that made
them sick at their stomachs, and they was right, but what they
meant by being tough was wrong . . . wrong because it was
sure as hell going to end them up in a worse mess than they
was in already.

Knowing how I used to be able to get the kids in my group
to sit down and talk over what was bugging them, I tried it
with Anthony, but I didn't get nowhere. If I hadn't been his
mama, maybe it would have worked better, or maybe nobody
could have gotten to him right then, I don't rightly know. He
wouldn't talk, and he wouldn't listen, not to me and not to
Guffy, just clammed up when we tried, and run out of the
house the first chance he got and stayed out as long as he
could. Worrying about him and worrying about how we
was going to live without me earning anything wasn't helping
me none, and I didn't seem to get any stronger, just at a time
when I needed my strength so bad.

Finally, Guffy, not being as bullheaded as I am, saw that
we couldn't make it, and he went down to the county to see
about getting help, and that's when we heard about Aid to
Dependent Children. Turned out that while Guffy earned
enough to pay for about six of us, he just couldn't make the

money stretch to cover all eleven, and since my first five was under age and not his own, the county helped by giving money to support them. It was a big relief to know there was something we could do, but the thought of going back on any kind of aid made me feel pretty bad, but there wasn't no choice. Since I was sick, the social worker come to the house, and I was surprised to see it was a man. He asked a lot of the same questions I was used to, poked around some, and said we'd be informed if our request had been approved. He wanted to know if we had enough money to eat on until the approval come through, 'cause there was a fund for emergencies that he could draw on if he had to. The way he said it, I was sure he was expecting me to say no, so I said yes, and then could have kicked myself, 'cause if the approval took more than a week we wasn't going to be eating too good, but I'm just naturally contrary and I have to pay for it.

Turned out, the approval took three weeks, and that last one was touch and go. We ended up eating beans most of the time, and the kids was pretty unhappy about it. Anthony just didn't come home for meals at all, and poor Jackie spent a lot of time out looking for him and mostly not doing too well. Guffy, who was usually there for me to lean on, was so mad at me for being bullheaded with the social worker that he couldn't hardly bring himself to talk to me, only had one thing to say, and that was, "You don't know the difference between pride and mule-pride. One comes from self-respect, the other comes from not having any. You knew damn well we didn't ask for no help until we did everything we could to help ourselves, so there wasn't no call for you to be ashamed and get your back up. Now your kids are paying for it."

I wanted to kill him. I felt bad enough without him rubbing it in, but he helped me to remember not to do it again, so I guess he knew what he was doing! Finally, we got the check, and it was pay day for Guffy besides, so we had a real meal for the first time in a couple of weeks. I made sure I told Anthony what we was going to have for dinner, but when it came time to eat he wasn't nowhere around, and all Guffy's searching didn't turn up any sign of him. By ten o'clock I was

getting pretty upset, and then the doorbell rung, and when I
opened it, there was Anthony and a policeman. My legs, which
weren't too strong yet anyhow, felt like they was turning to
water and I kind of hung on to the doorframe. The policeman kind of pushed Anthony in front of him and followed
him into the front room.

"You this kid's mother?" The policeman sat down on the
sofa and took out a little book and started writing in it.

"Yes, what's wrong?"

"He got a father?"

I nodded.

"Where is he?"

"Out looking for him."

"He wasn't doing much of a job."

"Please," I swallowed my anger, "what kind of trouble is he
in?"

"Car-stealing trouble."

It was so unexpected I almost laughed. Anthony was just
a little kid who was too big for his britches, but still a little
kid. How could he steal a car? He didn't even know how to
drive. It was silly, but it was the only thing I could think of,
so I said it.

"He didn't do the driving," the policeman replied. "His big-
shot friends did."

"Then how come he's the one you picked up?"

"Listen, don't get tough with me. You're damn lucky he's
here instead of down at Juvy with the rest of the rats he runs
with. The social worker down there talked the lieutenant into
letting him off 'cause he hasn't been in trouble before and he's
so much younger than the rest, but he ain't out of the woods
yet. You got to bring him down tomorrow morning at nine.
This is where you take him." He held out a card to me. My
hand was shaking so hard I almost dropped it, and the only
thing that kept me in one piece was hearing the front door
close and knowing Guffy had come back. The policeman repeated the same thing to him and then got up to leave.

"Seems like you people just don't give a damn about what
happens to your kids," he said, going out the door. Guffy

didn't say nothing, but I could feel what he was thinking, and as soon as we were alone, he sat Anthony down and really gave him hell. Being only twelve, Anthony was pretty scared at what had happened, and when he was scared he stopped trying to be tough and was just a kid again, and for the first time in a long time I saw the boy he used to be.

On account of his not being Guffy's natural child, I had to go downtown with him the next morning, and it took what little strength I had to do it. Turned out that Bill Wilson and some of his friends had decided to go joy-riding in a car they picked up somewhere, and they was cruising around when Anthony showed up. They pulled over and let him hop in, and then, after riding a few minutes more, they spotted a police car and got scared, 'cause they knew any policeman seeing a bunch of young black boys in a new car would pull them over. They turned a corner, parked, and all jumped out and ran, just ahead of the policemen . . . all but Anthony, that is. He was so scared he just sat there in the car, so of course they picked him up first. They got two of the others, but not Bill Wilson, who was more experienced at ducking, and hauled them and Anthony down to the station.

When we got down there the next morning, the judge conducting the hearing put Anthony on probation and told me that he was in my care, and if he got in trouble again he'd have to be sent to a foster home. I turned cold just hearing those words, and all the way home they went 'round and 'round in my head. I knew that Anthony was scared enough to behave for a little while, but what was to stop him from getting in trouble again when the scare wore off . . . and what was to stop my other kids, coming up in a neighborhood and a world like this one? I didn't know the answer, only that I had to try to do something about finding it out. I remembered the center in Cincinnati and the kids that came there and got a chance to talk and be listened to, and I figured maybe that was the place to begin, but I couldn't do it alone, so when I got home I went around to all the houses in my neighborhood that had young kids and I talked to their mothers. I asked them if they'd all come to a meeting at my house next night to talk about what we could do to help keep our kids out of trouble, and most of them not only agreed but asked if they could bring friends who didn't live around the block but had kids and were worried.

When the meeting got started, there were thirty women in my front room, instead of the eight or ten I had asked to come. I explained about the group work I had done back home, and one of the ladies suggested we try the same method. It sounded like a good idea, so I started it off by telling what had happened to Anthony and how scared I was that I couldn't stop it—or something worse—from happening again, and how maybe we could all help each other to help our kids. After about two hours of everybody telling their troubles, we made out a list of the things that most of the ladies agreed about, and it was something like this:

1. With most of the mothers out to work, the kids didn't have enough grown-up watching.
2. When they come home from school they went out on the street, and in a poor section of a big city the street wasn't no place for a kid to be.
3. All the mothers worked, but they didn't all work the same hours, so if we could get organized, we could have a list of mothers who could take turns running some kind of club the kids could go to.
4. To have a club, we had to have a place to meet, so we needed money for the place and for some equipment to put in it so we could keep the kids wanting to come there.
5. The government said it wanted to help keep kids off the street, and that's what we was talking about trying to do, so maybe the government would help us do it.

After we got the list finished, we decided that the first thing to do was to write a letter to Mr. Maldonado, who was the head of the poverty program, and they said since it was my idea to do something, I should start by doing that. So that's how I got started in community activities—in 1964.

It took me all of the next day to write the letter so's it

sounded right, but I finally got it done and sent it off, by air mail. We figured it would take a couple of days to get to Washington, and then maybe a couple more until it came to his attention, and then maybe three or four until he got around to answering it, and then it had to come from Washington back to L.A., and all that added up to at least two weeks. Then, being realistic, he might have more important things on his mind than a group of mothers on the outskirts of Watts, California, so we threw in another week or so and decided we could expect an answer within a month from the time I mailed the letter.

In the meantime, Ada Lennon, my next-door neighbor, suggested maybe we could use her yard and my yard and have a Sunday cook-out, and invite all the kids in the neighborhood who were between twelve and twenty, which were the ages we decided to include in our program. Anybody who had a little free time pitched in, everybody who had an extra dollar contributed it, and we even talked the grocery man into giving cans of beans and ears of corn and such, and we got together quite a feast. We put out the word that the eating was free and all you had to do to get in was be the right age, and then we just went ahead and cooked all the food we had, not knowing whether there'd be five kids or fifty, but hoping for the best.

It wasn't a big success, but it wasn't a big flop, neither. We started in about two o'clock in the afternoon, and the only kids who showed up until four were Ada's and mine and a couple who belonged to the block. Then at four or four thirty a bunch from another street come over to see what was going on and liked the way the barbecue smelled and so they stayed. Pretty soon a couple of gangs of tough-looking boys moseyed into the yard and just kind of hung around the edges, making jokes to each other and trying their damnedest to make it look like they wouldn't have nothing to do with such a stupid bunch of idiots. Just about then the second batch of hot dogs got done, so I put some on a big plate and kinda walked past where they was standing, letting them know they was welcome to eat if they were of a mind to. One of the biggest of them, who was the leader, I suppose, said, real snotty, "What time does the preaching start?"

"Whatever time you get to the church." I just kept walking, passing out the food.

"Ain't going to be no mealy-mouthed bastard telling us how we all going to end up in jail or worse?"

"Don't know what the point of that would be," I said, trying to keep a kid from taking three hot dogs in one hand, "since you already know it."

He didn't answer, but he took a hot dog, and when he did, I guess it was a signal to his gang that it was okay, and they all started to eat. Pretty soon some more kids come, and I got busy and didn't pay no mind for about an hour, and when I noticed them again, one of them had a harmonica and was playing, and some of the older boys and girls was dancing.

I guess the best thing that happened that day was that some of the kids who came expecting to laugh at us stayed and had a good time, so when we finally got organized with our Teen Post they was willing to come and give it a try. The ladies were real encouraged by the barbecue, and that kept them from losing interest when we didn't hear from Mr. Maldonado at all. Finally, after waiting for six weeks, I got mad. We kept hearing about how we should try to help ourselves, and here we was doing it and we couldn't even get an answer to a letter, so we held another meeting and decided to try again, this time writing directly to Sargent Shriver, who was the big name in the poverty program. I was elected to write again, and I did, and this time we got an answer in two weeks. Mr. Shriver's office said we should contact a Mr. Finley and a Mr. Robert Miller, who were in charge of the poverty program in L.A. It was time for a lesson in dealing with the government.

· 21 ·

BEFORE I KNEW WHAT HIT ME, I WAS MIXED UP IN INITIALS, meetings, and more meetings. It turned out that there had been some rough plans come down from Washington about starting what Mr. Miller called an umbrella service—a central meeting place where not only kids but adults and old people could come and get help of whatever kind they needed, but they was still just rough plans and nothing much was happening. I guess when I come in there with my list of needs from the ladies it was just the right time, and that's how the Teen Post got started.

First, we found a church in the area that was willing and able to let us use their meeting rooms for classes. Then, with the help of the local poverty program people and with money from the program, we were able to pay people to come in and teach classes in things like cooking, sewing, mechanics, workshop, and art, and we had dancing classes and sports and all manner of activities that interested the kids. The classes really were what we needed, 'cause they taught young people how to do things that could earn them some money, things that gave them the feeling that they could pull their own weight and take care of themselves, and the Teen Post helped adults because it paid them decent wages to help the kids.

I was the director of the post, and the money I earned helped so much at home that we was able to get off the county rolls, and when the people my age in the community saw that it was worthwhile to get involved in what was going on around them, they started coming to the meetings we had and generally taking an interest in what was going on. We organized a big clean-up campaign, got the kids to go around cleaning up empty lots and generally improve the looks of the neighborhood, and we got the mothers working on a schedule where there was always a couple of them around to keep an eye on the kids when they was out of school.

The greatest thing about what was going on was that although the government was helping with money, they was letting the people in the community help with everything else, and that way the money was getting into the hands of the people who needed it, and they was getting to be self-supporting and earning the right to self-respect. Pretty soon we outgrew the church 'cause we had so many things going on at once, and we was able to move to an empty commercial building with twice as many rooms. Everybody pitched in to clean up the place and move the equipment we had managed to get together over the year we had been functioning, and there was a real feeling of accomplishment when you walked through the front door. It was great, it really was, 'cause it was living proof that if the people in a black ghetto was given any hope of improving themselves and their homes, they had the drive and the gumption and the brains to start in and do it. We kept getting bigger and bigger and stronger and stronger, and we enlarged the services we did and had lots of the older kids planning to go on and be teachers so's they could come back to where they grew up and help other kids find themselves, too.

And then, at first so little that you hardly noticed, but getting bigger and bigger, we started to have problems about money. Seems like the poverty program was getting so complicated all over the country that the government felt it had to bring in a lot of professionals and experts to run it, and that was the beginning of the end for the people it was designed to help. It wasn't that these experts wasn't expert, they was; it was just that they wasn't poor and they didn't live with poverty every minute of every day of their lives, and they didn't really understand it. They didn't work with poor people, they worked with charts full of numbers that stood for poor people, and that's not the same thing by a long shot. The sociologists and the psychologists and the planners, looking at the statistics on drug users among the poor, decided that more money should go into programs designed to put a stop to that than should go into the classes we was holding, and little by little we had to drop them classes 'cause we couldn't pay the teachers. All of us who had been in our Teen Post from the beginning tried to get them to change their minds every way we could, all the way from letters and phone calls to organized marches on the state building and the federal offices, but it seemed like once the tide started to run the other way there wasn't no way to make it come back.

As usual, I was running myself ragged, but this time even Guffy didn't try to stop me, 'cause he felt what was going on was so important. I ran my house, and I ran the Teen Post, and I petitioned for funds, and I marched and I watched while the community that had been working together started to lose the faith they was just starting to get, and it like to broke my heart. Instead of listening, the government sent more and more experts to study what the other experts was doing wrong, and all the money that should have been going into the community was going into their pockets instead. I ain't meaning to say that they was doing it to be dishonest and I ain't meaning to say they didn't want to help us. I'm just saying that the only way to get people to help themselves is to let them. For a little while—almost a year and a half—they did let them, and the results was real good and would have gotten better, but it just didn't last long enough. When a people ain't had a break for a hundred years, it takes a little time to get them to seeing that they can change things for themselves by working and learning instead of by looting and burning, and that's what was happening in our community before the funds started getting thin.

I guess my strength was running out, and I know I was feeling pretty tired and discouraged, and I probably should have taken a rest, but it seemed like if I gave up then it would be a real defeat, not only for the kids in the neighborhood but for everything I set store by and tried to live by. One thing I had hollered at Connie I didn't have no right to say, 'cause I wasn't doing it myself, at least not then. I told him you had to try to change things, but when you couldn't change them you had to live so's you could respect yourself anyhow, and somehow, at that particular time, I had myself all mixed up with the Teen Post, so I felt if it failed then there wasn't no use trying to go on and make anything better ever. Feeling like that, I just naturally got sicker and sicker, until one day I passed out on the street in front of the Post and woke up in County General Hospital.

There was all kinds of things wrong with my insides from having so many kids and not ever giving myself a chance to get my strength back, and when they started trying to correct one thing, something else would give way, and I was sick for a long time, with "woman troubles" and with ulcers. At first, whenever Guffy come to see me I asked a million questions about the Post and how it was getting on, but after a while I stopped caring, 'cause I never heard anything good, and it was taking all the strength I could scrape up just to keep on living. I was in the hospital, off and on, for three months and laid up at home for a couple more and of course we ended up back on welfare and the Teen Post in our neighborhood finally closed.

When I was just about getting back on my feet, a lady from the poverty program come to the house and said even though our Post was closed that didn't mean they had forgotten what a good job I done, and I could be the director over to a center a few miles away. At first that made me feel good, and then when I checked in to it, it turned out they was going to fire somebody else who needed the job as much as I did to make room for me, and that just didn't make no sense.

I asked if they couldn't do without just one of the experts and that way have money to pay both of us, but they said it couldn't be done, and so I didn't go back to work. I heard later it wouldn't have made no difference anyhow, 'cause pretty soon they brought in a professional director and there wasn't no poor people left working in the center after that.

· 22 ·

It's been two years now since the teen post stopped being run by the people who needed to run it, and in those two years I been sick more than I been well, mainly with ulcers, so I've had to sit around a lot and think, and the more I think the more I know that both the government and the poor people need to believe in what my granddaddy used to say about self-reliance. It won't do no good at all to preach at people to help themselves if you keep stepping on their heads every time they manage to hold them up tall, but it won't do no good, neither, for the government to help get jobs for people who ain't trained for them and who feel that starting at the bottom is an insult.

There's so much talk lately about poverty and about black people—more talk than action—and it just don't seem possible that nobody's willing to listen to the poor, black and white, who know what's wrong and what it will take to make it right. If the government was to go into any poor community in the whole United States with the funds to back up its intentions, and if those funds was handled by a professional but all the other work was to be done by people who lived in the area,

222

and if those people was to be paid for their work on a realistic level, not too high and not too low, inside a year the relief rolls would be way down, the spirit of the community would be way up, and all the people involved would have learned valuable skills and lessons that they could then go and teach to others. It don't have to be as complicated as the experts say it is, I know that for a fact. They all got complicated minds, so they see things we don't, and sometimes those things hurt more than they help. On the other hand, when living revolves around earning enough money so's you can support your family and be a husband and a daddy who ain't ashamed to show his face around the house, it gets much simpler. It boils down to "teach me a trade, and then let me have a chance to work at what you taught me to do. I'll take it from there."

I think the history of the black woman in this country proves what I'm saying. From the time of slavery, the black woman was separated from her man, and the only thing she was taught was housework. Later, when she wasn't a legal slave no more and she had to get work 'cause her man couldn't, she set right out and did what she was trained for—housework. She didn't whine and cry and set home and starve, or steal and burn and generally raise a ruckus. Work was available, and maybe it wasn't the nicest or the best-paid but it was there to do, and she knew if she did it at least her family would eat.

It was a crime that black men was set free and then not taught anything they could do to earn money. It was a crime that they was treated like they was less than men just 'cause they was a different color. It was a crime that it took a super black man to do what an average white man could do, 'cause the white man made it that way. It was a crime that black kids mostly had to do their growing up in homes where their mothers were out working in other people's kitchens 'cause their fathers was denied a fair chance to get a job. It was a crime that in a rich country there was people starving or near starving for food and for self-respect. It was a crime that the black woman was forced to be mother, father, and breadwinner so much of the time. They was all crimes and they was wrong, evil, immoral, ungodly, and inhuman . . . but they happened, and we can't go back and make them un-happen. What we can do is see that they stop happening *now*.

Maybe we had to riot and burn so's they'd look at us. It ain't my way, and it ain't the way of a lot of folks I know, and in the long run it'll just get us all, rich and poor, black and white, a lot of trouble we don't need, but that's done, too. It's where we got to go from here that people should be thinking about, and by people I mean everybody from the President of the United States down through the middle class, black and white, to the poor, the sick, the aged. Ain't nobody I mentioned who ain't got a stake of some kind in what's going to happen, so they should be concerned.

Lord knows, I'm concerned. My neighbors are concerned. We tried to write down how we feel. Maybe you and your neighbors could do the same, and we could send all our thinking straight on to Washington. We think the government should enforce laws that outlaw segregation. We think that federal funds should be handled by experts but paid out to poor people on the basis of fair pay for a day's work done. We think education should be available to anybody who's willing to put in the effort to learn. We think that if industry wants good workers they should be willing to train them and get tax breaks if they do. We think that since so many boys and men have police records more as a result of the neighborhood they grew up in than as a result of their being no good, those police records should not stop them from getting a job. We think that all of us have to share in the responsibility of trying to turn out kids that respect the law because it's just, their parents because they're loving and fair, and themselves because they are willing to pay for what they get, so long as getting is possible. To do that, we can't start tomorrow. It will be too late.